SAINTS'
BLESSINGS

Text and art © 2004 by Meera Lester

First published in the USA in 2004 by
Fair Winds Press
33 Commercial Street
Gloucester, MA 01930

Library of Congress Cataloging-in-Publication Data
available

ISBN 1-59233-045-2

10 9 8 7 6 5 4 3 2 1

Cover design by Mary Ann Smith
Book design by Peter King and Company

Printed and bound in China

PERMISSIONS

From Andrews McMeel Publishing, Kansas City, Mo.,
for two excerpts from *Saintly Support: A Prayer for Every
Problem*, by Hope Gatto, copyright © 2003 by The Philip
Lief Group, Inc.

From Catholic Book Publishing Co., Totowa, N.J., for
excerpts from *The Confessions of St. Augustine*, revision of
the translation of Rev. J. M. Lelen, Ph.D. Reproduced
with permission from *The Confessions of St. Augustine*,
copyright © 1997 Catholic Book Publishing Co.,
Totowa, N.J. All rights reserved. For excerpts from
Treasury of Novenas, by Rev. Lawrence G. Lovasik.
Reproduced with permission from *Treasury of Novenas*,
copyright © 1986, Catholic Book Publishing Co.,
Totowa, N.J. All rights reserved.

From Charis, Ann Arbor, Mich., for excerpts from *A
Dictionary of Quotes from the Saints*, © 2001 by Paul
Thigpen. Published by Servant Publications, P.O. Box
8617, Ann Arbor, Michigan, 48107. Used with permission.

From Curtis Brown, Ltd., London, England, for excerpts
from *The Birth of Britain* (volume 1, History of the
English Speaking Peoples) by Winston S. Churchill,
copyright © 1962. Reprinted by permission of Curtis
Brown, Ltd.

From Doubleday, Division of Random House, New
York, N.Y., for excerpts from *Voices of the Saints, a Year of
Readings*, copyright © 2000 by Bert Ghezzi. Used with
permission.

From Glenstal Abbey, Limerick, Ireland, for excerpts
from *The Glenstal Book of Prayer, a Benedictine Prayer
Book*, copyright © 2001 by Glenstal Abbey.

From Penguin Putnam USA, Inc., New York, N.Y., for
excerpts from "Saints Joachim and Ann," "St Catherine
of Siena," "St. Francis of Assisi," "St. Maria Goretti," and
"St. Theresa of the Child Jesus," from *Novena, The Power
of Prayer*, by Barbara Calamari and Sandra DiPasqua,
copyright © 1999 by Barbara Calamari and Sandra
DiPasqua. Used by permission of Penguin, a
division of Penguin Group (USA), Inc.

SAINTS'
BLESSINGS

Wisdom and Guidance Inspired by
the World's Most Beloved Saints

TEXT AND ART BY MEERA LESTER

FAIR WINDS
PRESS
GLOUCESTER, MASSACHUSETTS

ACKNOWLEDGMENTS

The vision for this book came from my editor, Paula Munier, a beautiful spirit who has always exhibited great courage and passion for every endeavor she oversees or undertakes. After God, Mary, and the saints, I will always give Paula my undying devotion and friendship. Thank you, Paula.

For the inspiration for the art and many of the finer points of celebrating Catholicism, I am indebted to my Catholic traveling companion, Sadie Cabrera, whose ever-new joy at experiencing mass at different churches with me in tow has expanded my knowledge of the faith and opened my eyes and heart in new and blessed ways. Thank you, Sadie.

For her invaluable help in securing permissions and providing the kind of moral support that only one writer can give another, I wish to single out my dear friend and fellow author Anita Bronwyn Llewellyn—may we write forever and enjoy it always.

For her precision copyediting and project management skills, consummate professionalism, and enduring friendship, I am deeply grateful to Jan Stiles. Thank you, Jan.

I especially wish to thank Claire MacMaster, Holly Schmidt, Brigid Carroll, and everyone at Fair Winds involved in making this book possible.

Finally, I wish to offer up my heartfelt thanks to the saints (you know who you are) who inspired me as I wrote this book, rescued me on more than one occasion, and guided me in creating the images of saints in artwork. Thank you for leaving your indelible soul-prints in our collective consciousness.

Meera Lester

Author's Note

Great effort was made to verify the facts in this work; however, scholars sometimes disagree, and whenever such discrepencies arose in the biographical information for a particular saint's life, the interpretation of a majority of the sources was the one used in this book.

CONTENTS

INTRODUCTION

There are saints near you, as close as your breath. Beckon them to bless you. Don't be shy. They're waiting to help. Whisper a prayer. Have you lost something? Saint Anthony can help you find it. Are you battling a debilitating disease? With God's blessing, Saint Jude has worked many miracles. Are you hungry? Saint Anthony has fed countless souls, and Saint Vincent de Paul has clothed countless others. Do you wish you could be more loving? Saint John so loved God that he descended briefly into insanity.

In the following pages, you will find the stories of 36 saints who have experienced many of the same human challenges we face today. They dealt with spousal abuse, incest, mental illness, murder, mayhem, and more. From their exalted position in heaven, they are now available to help us if we but take the time to call upon them. From my own experiences, I have gained insights into how to pray to the saints as well as honor and venerate them, and I am thankful I can share what I've learned so that the saints may shower you with blessings as they have me, aiding me throughout my life.

Life for me was often difficult. I grew up in poverty on a Missouri farm. My mother once hammered kernels of corn gleaned from a gunnysack of chicken feed to make us a johnnycake—our meal that day. I had to chop wood, carry water and coal, and feed the chickens before breakfast. I had three stepfathers in short sequence, and

with one of them my mother had to work hard to eke out a living as a tenant farmer and later as a nurse's aid for the elderly. Early on, I hugged trees, long before this was considered a cool thing to do, and pretended they were holy beings. I considered Mother Nature my second mother, for I had not yet learned of Saint Thérèse of Lisieux, who called upon Mary to mother her after her earthly mother passed away. When I was still in grade school, I often slipped off to a field of tall grass, sank to my knees in the blazing hot sun, and begged God to save me. Would Saint Francis or Saint Clare have done otherwise?

As I grew into my late teens and early twenties, I developed a nighttime ritual that included reading about the lives of saints. After prayer, contemplation, and meditation, eventually sleep would follow. I found it deeply satisfying to know that these remarkable people once walked the earth and suffered many more travails than I ever would. They knew what I was going through. They knew how hard life could be. They knew how to turn inward and call upon the Lord's mercy and love. They could teach me how to rise above the stresses of life (and there always seemed to be so many) to a higher purpose—to open my heart and soul to the Holy Spirit.

As I bumped along the rocky road of my own life, I noticed that things often got a bit smoother when I took the time to ask for divine help. When money was tight,

Saint Anthony kept guiding me to the spaghetti dinners at Saint Lucy's—10 cents a dip. And friends, unaware that the cupboards at my house were bare, brought over frozen meals. But the biggest tests of my life and faith were yet to come, and for those I would need the intercession of the saints and God's infinite mercy.

Fate began lowering the proverbial boom when I was at last happily married with children of my own. My last stepfather died. Two weeks later, my sister died. A few months after that, my mother died of a massive heart attack. I cried out a fearful, heartfelt plea, "Please, God, don't take everyone from me." Then two more family members died, making a total of five in as many years. The death, the grief, and the foreboding that it was not yet "finished" tested my faith as never before.

Still, I continued my ritual of prayers, petitions, and loving praise of the saints, especially Mary, my favorite. But God wasn't through testing me. The biggest challenge was yet to come.

On a cold, dark February morning, a week before Valentine's Day, the heart of my 45-year-old husband, Steve, stopped beating in his sleep. I imagined the eyes of the Blessed Virgin, from their vantage point in the painting I had completed just days earlier, watching me pull Steve from our bed onto the floor and begin CPR. I wanted to cry, but I knew I couldn't allow that—not until the medics arrived and took over. I had to focus on correctly doing the compressions and breathing life-giving air into his lungs. My arms grew weary. Was it working? Would he live? Mary, Joseph, Jesus…please help me!

Mother Mary must have heard my cry. She knew what was in my heart, for hadn't I prayed the rosary and said other prayers each night just below her picture? Didn't I ask her to intercede to our Lord with my prayer, asking him to reverse my husband's heart ailment or to at least give us strength to deal with it?

Through the grace of God and surely the intercessory prayers of the blessed Mother Mary, my husband survived. We went on a second honeymoon to Hawaii. When we returned, he had a heart transplant. Then, 10 months later, he died. This time I truly experienced what Saint John of the Cross called the dark night of the soul. Tormented, alone, and suffering, I began to re-read the saints' stories for strength and inspiration. They got me through the agonizing weeks and months following Steve's death, and they continue to help me through the challenges of each new day. Writing this book is my way of saying thank you to all the saints, but especially to those who've helped me in my darkest hours. Life isn't easy for anyone, but with the saints' help, it doesn't have to be overwhelming.

The veneration of saints has been around since the second century. The first Christian saints were martyrs. They were buried, not cremated, and in most cases the day that they died and subsequently were born into their heavenly life is the day that is remembered, rather than their earthly birthday. Often, to mark this anniversary, a meal was served; thus the date became known as that saint's feast day. If a particular vocation, place, or struggle had some relevance to a saint's earthly existence, that saint might become its patron. Saint Luke, for example, is the patron saint of doctors because he was a doctor, while Saint Francis of Assisi is the patron saint of ecology and animals because of his reverence for the land and all its creatures. Saint Francis is also the patron saint of Italy, a distinction he shares with Saint Catherine of Siena.

The saints are sanctified (the Latin term *sanctus* means holy) and stand as models of virtue for us to emulate. Though they dwell in heaven, they are also ever near and accessible.

WHO WERE THE SAINTS?

The saints in this book were ordinary people who were called to an extraordinary life in God. While some became martyrs, others were contemplatives, founders of religious orders, or theologians. Some started out life in poverty while others were born into wealth. Some were virgins and others were married with families. But all heeded an inner call to live a highly virtuous and holy life in service to God and his children. They dedicated their incarnations on Earth to doing God's will so that in the eternal life they could be united with him. What

does this mean for the ordinary person in the twenty-first century? You can invoke the saints' blessings for your own life. You can call on the saints to pray to God with you and to offer their own prayers of holy intensity to him on your behalf.

HOW DOES SOMEONE BECOME A SAINT?

The road to sainthood is not an easy one. After the first few centuries, when people could achieve sainthood by virtue of living a holy life and subsequently having their popularity grow into a cult after their death, the Catholic Church established a rigorous system for determining who could become a saint. While there are three basic steps to sainthood—beatification, canonization, and sainthood—it is first necessary for an advocate to submit a person's name for consideration. If the nominee's life stands up to scrutiny, if others can say for certain that this individual lived a virtuous and holy life or died a martyr, and if all agree that consideration is justified, the candidate is declared "venerable."

Once a person has been nominated and determined to have lived a holy life, actual beatification can happen only with the approval of the cardinals of the Congress for the Causes of Saints. For beatification to be approved, two miracles must have occurred as a direct result of people's prayers asking the potential saint to intercede for them after his or her death. Once this step has been passed, the candidate is called "blessed." Then one more miracle

must take place before the pope can canon-
ize someone and declare this person a saint.
For the canonization of martyrs, however,
no miracles are needed.

HOW DO YOU OPEN YOURSELF TO THE SAINTS' BLESSINGS?

If you are not able to walk any of the
saints' particular life paths, you can certainly
enjoy the remarkable stories of their lives
and be inspired by them. At the end of
each saint's story, you will find specific
things you can do to venerate and honor
that saint. You will also find prayers or
novenas to enable you to petition that
saint. For some saints, there are additional
ways to celebrate their lives and call forth
their blessings, such as making a pilgrimage,
creating sacred art, or preparing a special
type of food for that saint's feast day.

A bedtime ritual that includes reading,
meditation, contemplation, and invitation
to the saints and God to come into your
heart, can open you to insights, forgiveness,
blessings, and beautiful dreams. You can
also make a deliberate effort each day to
empty your consciousness of ego, vanity,
and pride to embrace the kind of poverty
that Hildegard addressed and Saint John of
the Cross espoused. This regular emptying
of self enables you to become increasingly
comfortable with looking inward for
divinely inspired insights and communion
with the Lord. In this way, you learn to live
an inner-directed life outwardly in the
world. This is what the saints learned to do,
and this is one of the reasons why their
incarnations on earth remain so meaningful
and relevant today.

May you be drawn into the stories of these
remarkable lives and, through your prayers
and petitions, be showered with God's great
mercy and love, and with the saints' blessings.

*Dedicated to Christ's mother Mary, Queen
of Heaven and most exalted of all the saints
and to my mother Elizabeth Louise.*

THE WOMAN WHO STAYED BEHIND [AT THE TOMB] TO SEEK CHRIST
WAS THE ONLY ONE WHO SAW HIM. FOR PERSEVERANCE IS ESSENTIAL
TO ANY GOOD DEED. AS THE VOICE OF TRUTH TELLS US: "WHOEVER
PERSEVERES TO THE END WILL BE SAVED."

— POPE GREGORY THE GREAT

SAINT AGATHA

It is easy to believe that we will stick to our promises and principles as long as they aren't challenged. But how much more difficult it is to remain steadfast and persevere when we are tested or tortured for our beliefs and convictions as was Saint Agatha in the third century.

Born into nobility and raised in Catania, Sicily by parents who were Christians, Agatha had everything a girl could want—beauty, money, and property. When her mother and father passed away, Agatha was left materially endowed but bereft of the love and guidance only parents can give.

While several young men may have had eyes just for her, one individual in particular was obsessed with claiming her as his wife. Quintianus, the Roman consul of Sicily, seemingly had an obsessive and sadistic streak. He devised a scheme. Using a decree by the Roman emperor opposing Christians, he would order Agatha to appear before him. That done, he proposed marriage, but she promptly declined, saying she had already pledged her virginity to Christ. This declaration, along with her unwillingness to denounce her religion, infuriated Quintianus. He ordered her to be taken to a brothel where she was forced to live as a prostitute

for a month. Agatha wept, prayed, and suffered miserably in that environment. She wished for martyrdom.

Aphrodisia, the woman who ran the brothel, eventually explained to Quintianus that it seemed unlikely that Agatha would turn away from her Christian beliefs. Quintianus then ordered Agatha's body to be laid upon a rack, bound, and tortured. Angered that Agatha could withstand the persecution and still invoke Christ as her savior, Quintianus ordered her breasts first crushed and then amputated. She was thrown in a prison cell without nourishment or medical attention for her mutilation.

Still, Agatha did not despair or turn away from her belief. Steadfast in her faith, she experienced a sacred vision of Saint Peter, and God healed her and restored her breasts during the night.

Quintianus, unimpressed with her miraculous healing, proclaimed that the defiant Agatha be stripped naked and rolled on pottery shards and smoldering coals. Just as his orders were being carried out, the earth began to shake. People of Catania scattered in every direction, seeking escape and screaming that the earthquake was Quintianus' fault. Quintianus tried to save himself but died in his attempt.

Lived–Third century
Martyred–Virgin martyr, A.D. 251
Feast day–February 5
Patron saint of bell-founders, breasts, nurses, firefighters, and foundry workers

Agatha, it is said, begged to be allowed to join Christ in heaven. She passed away in prison as a result of her suffering, and someone covered her body with a veil (or possibly a death shroud).

Almost immediately, miracles and healing began to take place. In the year after Agatha's entombment, Mount Etna erupted. Believers in the virgin martyr prayerfully attached her veil to a staff and waved it before the mountain. Incredibly, the flow of lava stopped and the mountain became quiet. Since then, Agatha has been invoked to intercede against volcanic eruptions, earthquakes, and diseases of the breasts. Even today, the people of Catania celebrate her feast day by carrying her veil on a staff during a procession through the city. In this way they honor and celebrate the saint's holy convictions and invoke her blessings.

In art, Agatha is often pictured holding her breasts on a platter or tray. ✛

WAYS TO HONOR AND INVOKE THE BLESSINGS OF SAINT AGATHA

✛ Make a pilgrimage to Catania for Agatha's feast day. Participate in the holy festivities.

✛ Create a Saint Agatha medal using polymer clay. Since, of course, there are no photographs of her, you may want to photocopy an image or do a miniature pen-and-ink drawing. Transfer or impress the image onto polymer clay. Fit the clay inside a small, metal aspirin box (cutting away excess clay), and bake according to the clay manufacturer's instructions. Paint the box and then glue a pin or clip to the back. Remember that the medal is just a medal until it is blessed and infused with the love and faith that you bear for the saint. Have a priest bless it for you.

✛ Perform a prayerful and loving act of kindness for someone suffering from breast cancer.

✛ Pray Saint Agatha's prayer for patients and give a copy of it to a person battling breast cancer.

✛ Imagine you are creating in the temple of your heart a beautiful, sacred space for the Lord and his saints. Visualize your heart with golden doors that open onto a tranquil garden or some other lovely setting. Make an imaginary bouquet with exquisite flowers and offer them to the Lord.

✝ Breathe deeply and slowly; then relax. Imagine your body being filled with the healing light of God. Imagine that every cell, bone, muscle, and organ exists in a state of perfection. You feel the warmth of the sun and the bliss of the divine comforter intoning a healing hymn throughout your being. Disease cannot exist here. You are healthy and whole.

AFFIRMATIONS

I forgive those who have violated me.

I invite the Lord to enter through the sacred doorway of my heart to commune with me.

I listen to the Holy Spirit for guidance in the ways to become healed and whole again.

I am being healed through the power of God's love.

I am sending the love he expresses through me into the world to heal others.

Novena to Saint Agatha

O Saint Agatha, who withstood unwelcome advances from unwanted suitors, and suffered pain and torture for your devotion to our Lord, we celebrate your faith, dignity, and martyrdom.

Protect us against rape and other violations, guard us against breast cancer and other afflictions of women, and inspire us to overcome adversity.

O Saint Agatha, virgin and martyr, mercifully grant that we who venerate your sacrifice may receive your intercession. Amen.

Recite this novena nine times in a row for nine days in a row.

— CALAMARI AND DIPASQUA, 1999

Breast Cancer Patients' Prayer to Saint Agatha

Pure maiden of Sicily,

You were tortured to the core of your womanhood.

Pray that I have the same courage as I fight the raging battle within my body.

In the Lord's name, ask that I may be brave in this struggle,

Strong in will and determined in spirit in the face of illness.

Let me remember your sturdiness when I am feeling weak. Amen.

— PHILIP LIEF GROUP, INC., 2003

INSPIRED WITH THIS CONFIDENCE, I COME BEFORE YOU SINFUL AND SORROWFUL. HOLY MOTHER OF THE IMMACULATE VIRGIN MARY AND LOVING GRANDMOTHER OF THE SAVIOR, DO NOT REJECT MY APPEAL, BUT HEAR ME AND ANSWER MY PRAYER. AMEN.

— MEMORARE TO SAINT ANN

SAINT ANN

For many couples who are infertile, the sadness caused by not being able to have a child together can really be understood only by those who have gone through that experience themselves. Saint Ann and Saint Joachim, her husband, were such a couple.

What great faith Ann must have exhibited to earn God's favor and the blessing of a much longed-for pregnancy. God kept his promise. Saint Ann would have to keep her word to God as well. She and her husband had promised that if God would give them a baby, they would consecrate the child to God.

Ann was the mother of Mary and grandmother of Jesus. Yet not much is known about this holy woman. There is no mention of her in the Bible. Because she was unable to have children, Ann had likely resigned herself to dying barren. Just imagine how utterly shocked and overjoyed she must have been, after having prayed so long and earnestly without response, to receive at midlife the news that God would not only grant her petition but bless her with the privilege of birthing and rearing a special, sacred daughter. What if Ann had given up, stopped believing, stopped praying?

Ann (also called Hannah or Anna) was raised in a Jewish family in the town of Nazareth and wed Joachim when she was about 20. Though they both wanted children—and were expected in their society to have a family—they remained barren for decades and were publicly chastised for it. When Ann reached the age of 40 and Joachim was 69, Joachim went into the desert to fast and pray for 40 days, leaving Ann at home. The angel of God appeared to them simultaneously and conveyed the news that Ann would bear a child. They would name her Mary, the angel said, and she would be known throughout the world.

Since the couple had vowed that if they were given a child, they would consecrate that child to the temple, Ann and Joachim surrendered Mary when she turned three. Mary, thereafter, lived a sheltered, religious life, learning to love and serve God. As for Ann, the inevitable ups and downs of motherhood were nothing compared to the opposing emotions of elation and sadness from knowing that she would suckle and nurture her child just a short time and then be obliged to hand her over to someone else's care. But through the grace of God, Ann never wavered in her commitment.

Lived–First century
Feast day–July 26
Patron saint of Canada, mothers and children, homemakers, miners, cabinetmakers, housewives, pregnant women, women in labor, and those who are infertile

Saint Ann has been loved through the centuries. Churches have been built in her honor, and her relics have been placed in Jerusalem, Rome, and Apt-in-Provence. In art images, she is often depicted with Mary in a motherly role of teacher (teaching Mary to read) or shown with her husband, Saint Joachim. ✢

WAYS TO HONOR AND INVOKE THE BLESSINGS OF SAINT ANN

✢ Make a sacred box and decorate it as beautifully as you can with holy images, beautiful paper, and scriptural verses written in gold pen. Throughout your week, as inspiration moves you, write prayers, messages, and thank-you notes to Ann concerning your home, your marriage, your parenting, and your life as a woman loving God. Keep them in your sacred box.

✢ Think of something that you very much want God to manifest in your life. Be willing to give it up. Pray Saint Ann's novena to ask her intercessory help.

✢ Incorporate the color blue in areas where you pray or read Scripture. Blue is the color most often associated with both Saint Ann and Mother Mary.

✢ Attempt to keep your house in perfect order, as Saint Ann did, or at least make it a place that warmly welcomes loved ones, friends, and visitors as well as the holiest of the holy.

✢ Donate some time each week to doing something special for grandparents. If yours are no longer alive, consider volunteering at a senior center.

Novena to Saint Ann

Glorious Saint Ann, I desire to honor you with special devotion. I choose you after the Blessed Virgin as my spiritual mother and protectress. To you I entrust my soul and my body, all my spiritual and temporal interests, as well as those of my family.

To you I consecrate my mind, that in all things it may be enlightened by faith; my heart, that you may keep it pure and fill it with love for Jesus, Mary, Joseph, and yourself; my will, that like yours, it may always be one with the Will of God.

Good Saint Ann, filled with love for those who invoke you and with compassion for those who suffer, I confidently place before you my earnest petition (mention your request).

I beg you to recommend my petition to your daughter, the Blessed Virgin Mary, that both Mary and you may present it to Jesus. Through your earnest prayers may my request be granted. But if what I ask for should not be according to the Will of God, obtain for me that which will be for the greater benefit of my soul. By the power and the grace with which God has blessed you, extend to me your helping hand.

But most of all, merciful Saint Ann, I beg you to help me master my evil inclinations and temptations, and to avoid all occasions of sin. Obtain for me the grace of never offending God, of fulfilling faithfully all the duties of my state of life, and of practicing all those virtues that are needed for my salvation.

Like you, may I belong to God in life and in death through perfect love. And after having loved and honored you on earth as a truly devoted child, may I, through your prayers, have the privilege of loving and honoring you in heaven with the Angels and Saints throughout eternity.

Good Saint Ann, mother of her who is our life, our sweetness and our hope, pray to her for me and obtain my request. Amen.

Recite this novena nine times in a row for nine days in a row.

— LOVASIK, 2000

POVERTY IS TRUE RICHES. SO PRECIOUS IS POVERTY THAT GOD'S
ONLY-BEGOTTEN SON CAME ON EARTH IN SEARCH OF IT.
IN HEAVEN HE HAD A SUPERABUNDANCE OF ALL GOODS. NOTHING
WAS LACKING THERE BUT POVERTY.

— SAINT ANTHONY OF PADUA

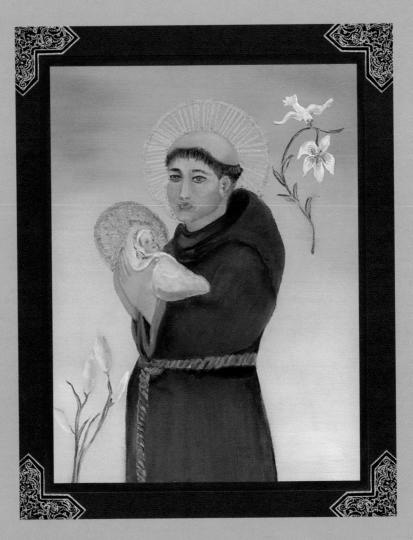

SAINT ANTHONY OF PADUA

Poverty is a terrible thing for anyone to endure, especially a child. In many parts of the world today, including the United States, many mothers work two jobs to put a meager meal on the table. Fathers feel ashamed that they can't find work or provide shelter for their families, and too many children start and end the day with empty stomachs.

Saint Anthony looked into the face of poverty throughout his life. During the Middle Ages, he comforted the poor with the words of the Lord and soothed their hunger with nourishment for the body. Mercy, intercession, love of the poor, spiritual renewal—all these virtues are associated with him. He made sure his example matched his words. May we be inspired by his example to love and care for the poor throughout the year, not just during holidays.

Born into a noble Portuguese family in Lisbon, Anthony was baptized Ferdinand. His parents entrusted their son's education to clergy members of the Cathedral of Lisbon. He later transferred to the regular canons of Saint Augustine and, two years after that, switched to the priory at Coîmbra, in those days the capitol of Portugal.

After several years there, he became inspired by the martyrdom in Morocco of some Franciscans whose relics had been brought to Coîmbra. It was then that Ferdinand decided he too wanted to be a soldier for Christ. He knew he was prepared to lay down his life. He bared his soul to some visiting Franciscans, and in 1221 they allowed him to enter their order. He changed his name to Anthony.

In due time he sailed to Ceuta and was set to leave for Morocco but was waylaid by severe illness. He took a boat back to Europe, only to land in Sicily after the boat was blown off course. From there, he traveled to Assisi, where a great assembly was about to take place. Saint Francis himself would be there. Anthony attended the event, which was undoubtedly a pivotal point in his life.

Lived–A.D. 1195–1231
Feast day–June 13
Special titles–Evangelical Doctor, Saint of Miracles, Wonderworker of Padua
Patron saint of Portugal, lost objects, poor and oppressed people, barren women, amputees, animals, expectant mothers, fishermen, mail, mariners, pregnant women, sailors, travelers, American Indians, and the elderly

He was then assigned to a post in San Paolo, a little town near Forli, where his eloquence, theological and biblical learning, and speaking powers astounded everyone. News of the gifts of this young friar spread, and soon he was reassigned to preach throughout central Italy. It's been noted that Saint Francis himself gave Anthony his assignment to teach theology within the community.

Sometime after 1226, Anthony took up residence at Padua. Exhausted from preaching, hearing confessions, and other work, Anthony sought retreat in a place known as Camposanpiero. As he continued to grow weaker, however, he asked to return to Padua. On June 13, 1231, Anthony died at the age of 36. His body lies in the basilica of Saint Anthony in the church of Our Lady in Padua. He was canonized in 1232 and declared a Doctor of the Church in 1946 by Pope Pius XII.

Anthony became known as the patron saint of lost objects after a young monk borrowed or stole his beloved Psalter. When the book could not be found, Anthony said prayers, and a frightening apparition suddenly appeared before the young monk, ordering him to return the Psalter to its rightful owner.

Anthony felt a deep devotion to the poor. Long after his death, he became the namesake of the charitable institution Saint Anthony's Bread. The idea behind bread for the poor arose from a miracle that took place after the work on the basilica of Saint Anthony was completed. A small child who was left near a container of water fell in and drowned. His mother prayed fervently to Saint Anthony and offered to distribute her child's weight in bread to the poor if only her little one could recover. Miraculously, the child did. This miracle evolved into a devotion called *pondus pueri*, or the weight of a child, for charitable giving.

In churches today, next to images of Saint Anthony there is often a collection box, or "poor box," with this inscription: "Saint Anthony's Bread." On Saint Anthony's feast day in Sicily, enormous loaves of bread are formed in the shape of a crown and baked. In art, Anthony is often shown with his beloved Psalter, lilies for purity, and the infant Jesus. ✣

WAYS TO HONOR AND INVOKE THE BLESSINGS OF SAINT ANTHONY

✢ Read biographies of Saint Anthony's life, such as *Saint Anthony, Doctor of the Church* by Sophronius Clasen (Franciscan Herald Press, 1987).

✢ Pick an ordinary day of the week and go shopping, not for your own family but for God's family of the poor. Donate your sack of groceries to a local food bank or charity.

✢ Perform an act of random kindness and tell no one about it. God knows the instant you do it. No one else needs to know.

✢ Check out the monthly magazine of the Franciscan friars, *Saint Anthony Messenger*, at www.AmericanCatholic.org. Find and read any of Claude Jarmak's translations of Saint Anthony's prayers and sermons, including *Praise to You Lord: Prayers of Saint Anthony*. Find information on these items at http://franinst.sbu.edu/filib/people/anthony_of_padua.htm.

✢ Buy a Saint Anthony religious candle, place it on your altar, and say his novena. For an offering of $4 or more, you can obtain for your altar a medal containing a bit of cloth touched to the relic of the uncorrupted tongue of Saint Anthony. Write to Franciscan Mission Associates, Box 598, Mt. Vernon, NY 10551. Perpetual novenas to Saint Anthony are often said on Tuesdays.

Novena to Saint Anthony

O Holy Saint Anthony, glorious for the fame of your miracles, obtain for me from God's mercy this favor that I desire: (mention your request).

Since you were so gracious to poor sinners, do not regard my lack of virtue but consider the glory of God which will be exalted once more through you by the granting of the petition that I now earnestly present to you.

Glorious Wonderworker, Saint Anthony, father of the poor and comforter of the afflicted, I ask for your help. You have come to my aid with such loving care and have comforted me so generously. I offer you my heartfelt thanks.

Accept this offering of my devotion and love and with it my earnest promise which I now renew, to live always in the love of God and my neighbor. Continue to shield me graciously with your protection, and obtain for me the grace of being able one day to enter the kingdom of heaven, there to praise with you the everlasting mercies of God. Amen.

— LOVASIK, 2000

THE NIGHT IS FAR SPENT, THE DAY IS AT HAND:
LET US THEREFORE CAST OFF THE WORKS OF DARKNESS,
AND LET US PUT ON THE ARMOUR OF LIGHT.

— ROMANS 13:12

SAINT AUGUSTINE OF HIPPO

What is there to fear, Paul wrote in his epistle to the Romans, once we've put on the armor of light? The imagery of light emanating from Jesus suggests an illumination that can not be penetrated by darkness. There is light to be found within us as we learn to turn inward and seek the bidding of God.

Augustine, during his lifetime, struggled against the darkness within himself. While he longed for truth eloquently spoken, for reason, and for light, he also fought a constant battle against his strong sexual desires. In his *Confessions*, written much later in life, he called himself a sinner who engaged in sexual immorality from the age of 17. How human he becomes through his words: "Give me chastity and continence, but not for a while." (Lelen, 1997)

As he struggled in one of those dark nights of the soul that each of us, at one point or another, seems to pass through, Augustine ran into a garden and threw himself upon the ground beneath the canopy of a fig tree.

There he cried out in desperation, asking the Lord why he did not just instantly put an end to his uncleanness.

Lived–A.D. 354–430
Feast day–August 28
Special titles–Doctor of the Church, Bishop of Hippo, Doctor of Grace
Patron saint of England, theologians, printers, and brewers

"How long, O Lord, will You be angry forever? Remember not our former iniquities." (Lelen, 1997)

Sometime during this emotional outburst, Augustine claimed to hear a child (he could not discern whether a boy or a girl) chanting in a singsong voice the words "Tolle, lege" (Latin for "pick up, read"). He interpreted the words as a divine admonition to pick up the Bible and read. Augustine ran to the place where he'd left his Bible lying just moments before. He began to read: "Let us walk honestly, as in the day: not in rioting and drunkenness, not in chambering and wantonness, not in strife and envying. But put ye on the Lord Jesus Christ, and make not provision for the flesh, to fulfil the lusts thereof." (Romans 13:13–14)

Augustine had no need to read further. In those words, he immediately experienced a life-altering shift in his heart and mind. He'd opened the door and the light streamed in.

Aurelius Augustinus was born on November 13, A.D. 354, in North Africa near Hippo. His family was neither rich nor poor. His father, a pagan and idolater, possessed darkly violent tendencies, while his mother Monica was a strong-willed Christian woman. Augustine's mother taught him her Christian beliefs and how to pray. She couldn't know what a wayward boy he would become.

An exemplary student, Augustine applied himself to the study of law and writing. His life, unhampered by the need for money, was one of sin and sensuality. He took a mistress and had a son when he was 18. Fascinated by the mystery of evil, he embraced Manichaeism, a belief system that holds that the universe is under the dominion of two opposing principles: good and evil. His sharp mind grappled with the ideas of Manichaeism for some time before moving on to other intellectual pursuits. Eventually, Augustine left Africa and moved to Rome with his mistress and their young son.

Augustine pursued his own studies and taught rhetoric for a while before moving again, this time to Milan. Sometime during this phase of his life, he sent his mistress back to Africa. His mother, ever resolute in her determination to see her errant son on the right path to God and finally baptized, was waiting for him in Milan. It was a jubilant day for Monica when the bishop of Milan, Saint Ambrose, baptized the 33-year-old Augustine and his son in A.D. 387 on the eve of Easter. That she would live to see Augustine find salvation was something Monica was promised in a vision. A few months later, while she and Augustine were en route to North Africa, she fell ill and died.

Augustine completed the journey home to the town of his birth, Tagaste. Around A.D. 389, his teenage son also died. Two years later, Augustine was ordained and began the work of teaching and preaching. He quickly gained a following because of his charismatic and compelling style. Like Saint Anthony of Padua after him, he resorted to preaching in large public meeting areas rather than churches to accommodate the crowds who gathered to hear him.

After serving one year as co-adjutor to the bishop of Hippo, Augustine himself became bishop. He died on August 28, A.D. 430, after Hippo had been under siege for three months, attacked by men fighting under the authority of the King of the Vandals, who had chosen to invade the African provinces. By that time, Augustine had spent roughly 40 years in the service of the ministry. His critical thinking and reasoning can be seen in his prolific writings, including the dialogues (*Of the Happy Life, Of Order*, and *Against the Academicians*) and books (*On the Trinity*, *City of God*, and *Confessions*, his most famous). Because Augustine wrote openly about his all-too-human struggles with the pleasures of the flesh, many people find inspiration in his life story.

… being placed as I am in the midst of these temptations, I engage in a struggle every day against concupiscence in eating and drinking. This is not something I can resolve to cut off once and for all and touch no more, as I could do with regard to concubinage. The reins that restrain the throat must be held neither too loosely nor too tightly.

—SAINT AUGUSTINE (LELEN, 1997)

Augustine's writing reflects his belief that the life of man upon earth is all trial and that one's only hope is in God's mercy. Like Matthew, he turned to the light: "The light of the body is the eye: if therefore thine eye be single, thy whole body shall be full of light. But if thine eye be evil, thy whole body shall be full of darkness. If therefore the light that is in thee be darkness, how great is that darkness!" (Matthew 6:22–23) ✠

WAYS TO HONOR AND INVOKE THE BLESSINGS OF SAINT AUGUSTINE

✠ Read Augustine's own works, such as *The Confessions of Saint Augustine*, revised translation by the Reverend J. M. Lelen (Catholic Book Publishing Company, 1997), and biographies of his life, such as *Saint Augustine* by Garry Wills (Viking, 1999), to get an idea of how this man used his God-given gift of a fine mind to discern truth, to teach, and to preach.

✠ Claim a period of silence for yourself sometime during the day. Say a prayer, and in the silence afterward wait for spirit to fill the emptiness. If you feel inspired, write a poem or essay about your own struggle with darkness and light.

✠ Vow to swim against the current instead of just floating downstream through life. Make an effort to go in the opposite direction—upstream, ever toward God. Conversion, Saint Augustine believed, was nothing less than a lifelong process. Struggle, as this saint did, to win the battle against the darkness around you and in you. Learn to control your senses, or they will become that which controls you. Ask for Saint Augustine to pray with you to ask the Lord's help in your ongoing effort to live a more spirit-filled life.

Prayer to Saint Augustine

O Saint Augustine, inspire all seeking to overcome darkness in their lives and who are in need of the grace of our Lord. Through many years of struggle, you at last saw the light. Inspired by your example, I implore you to intercede for me to our Lord to help me overcome my temptations and adversities and to live with an awareness of God as my constant companion and source of all light in my life. The gratitude of my heart will ever be with you. Amen.

. . . LAY UP FOR YOURSELVES TREASURES IN HEAVEN, WHERE
NEITHER MOTH NOR RUST DOTH CORRUPT, AND WHERE THIEVES DO
NOT BREAK THROUGH NOR STEAL: FOR WHERE YOUR TREASURE IS, THERE
WILL YOUR HEART BE ALSO.

— MATTHEW 6:19–21

SAINT BERNADETTE SOUBIROUS

Trust, integrity, and simplicity are qualities worthy of cultivation in our lives. Consider their opposites: dishonesty, unscrupulousness, and complexity—these attributes could describe any criminal serving time, couldn't they? Yet can any of us really look into the mirror of self-examination and swear that we've never been dishonest (yes, little white lies count) or unscrupulous? In terms of vanity, wouldn't we prefer to see ourselves as complex rather than simple? Yet trust, integrity, and simplicity are closer to that pure innocence of children that Jesus and his mother so loved. These were also the qualities of Saint Bernadette Soubirous. She would need them to withstand the firestorm of interrogations levied at her to test her credibility.

Young Bernadette Soubirous was not endowed with a strong body, a sharp mind, the gift of eloquence, or any of the other qualities associated with many of the saints. Yet, by the age of 14, she was blessed to have witnessed 18 visions of the Virgin Mary at the Rock of Massabielle, Lourdes. Bernadette was the oldest of six children born to the French miller François Soubirous. Living in abject poverty, she suffered from various ailments, including asthma.

Lived–A.D. 1844–1879
Canonized–1933
Feast day–April 16
Patron saint of shepherds

While hunting for firewood on February 11, 1858, she had a vision of the Blessed Mother, who subsequently referred to herself as the Immaculate Conception. Only a few years prior to Bernadette's vision, the dogma regarding Mary, mother of Jesus, having been conceived without original sin (the Immaculate Conception) had been put forth and defined by Pope Pius IX.

The Virgin Mary offered a simple message: Do penance for the conversion of sinners and encourage people to come and pray at the place where the apparitions are occurring. She directed Bernadette to the site of a hidden spring and told her to drink and bathe in it. She also told Bernadette that a church should be built over the site. Several sources note that the once hidden spring now produces 27,000 gallons of water each day.

As news of that heavenly apparition and subsequent ones spread to the community and beyond, people began to openly seek the healing power of the water. Lourdes became a major pilgrimage destination— the most popular in Europe.

Bernadette, however, had to endure rigorous questioning from skeptical members of the clergy and civic leaders. Because she was uneducated, some nonbelievers suggested she'd made everything up. Yet Bernadette never wavered. She joined the Sisters of Notre Dame of Nevers in 1866, changing her name to Maria Bernarda. Just 10 years later, the new basilica in Lourdes opened.

Bernadette did not attend. Three years after that, at age 35, Bernadette died from a protracted battle with tuberculosis of the bones.

Over the years, her body was exhumed three times, first to identify her relics, second as part of the process of canonization, and finally to send her relics to Rome and to the houses of the Sisters of Nevers throughout the world. At each exhumation, her body was found incorrupt, without any sign of decay. She was canonized not because of her mystical visions but rather, as her hagiographers have noted, because of her simplicity of faith, integrity, and enduring perseverance.

Today, the still incorrupt body of Saint Bernadette lies in the main chapel of the Convent of Saint Gildard in Nevers, France. Inscribed around her shrine is the promise made to her by the Most Blessed Virgin: "I do not promise that you will be happy in this world, only in the next." ✢

WAYS TO HONOR AND INVOKE THE BLESSINGS OF SAINT BERNADETTE

✢ Rent and watch the movie *Song of Bernadette*, based upon the life of Bernadette Soubirous.

✢ Keep a rosary in your pocket so that whenever you are inclined to pray, whether you're doing tasks like Bernadette's gathering of firewood or picking up groceries for dinner, you have only to touch it to become inspired and begin praying.

✢ Make a pilgrimage to Lourdes. Participate in the holy activities.

✢ Obtain some holy water from Lourdes (for a donation, holy water can be ordered in the United States through the Oblates of Mary Immaculate, National Shrine of our Lady of the Snows in Belleville, Illinois). Share it with those who desperately need it.

✢ Use religious objects, ribbon, your own spiritual writing or a copy of a prayer to Saint Bernadette, and photographs or an art image of her to create a small shrine to honor this saint who neither wanted nor sought to be the focus of the throngs of curious followers drawn by her visions of the blessed Virgin Mary.

✛ Breathe in and out three times, releasing all the tension in your body. Ponder the following: My work becomes sacred work when I set aside my ego, let go of the need for recognition, and understand that the Lord is the real doer performing his work through my body and mind. To him belongs the glory for all my accomplishments.

✛ Offer yourself and the skills you have to advance the work of the Lord and his mother. Consider that the Blessed Virgin chose to reveal herself 18 times, not to a brilliant scholar, eloquent statesman, or beautiful model, but to a poor, illiterate, asthmatic girl. What sacred gifts might you offer to the world?

AFFIRMATIONS

I embrace the uniqueness of my body, mind, and accomplishments.

I celebrate my God-given attributes and abilities.

I am thankful for the successes of my endeavors.

POEM FROM THE VISIONARY OF LOURDES TO THE IMMACULATE CONCEPTION

What matter the length of day, the cycle of season.
I thought my work was gathering firewood.
Like a zephyr you caressed my consciousness,
Filling my world with awe and light.
I let go of the kindling and reached for the flame.

Prayer to Saint Bernadette

O Saint Bernadette, I seek your intercession and ask you to present my petitions to our Lord Jesus Christ. Inspired by your suffering and devotion to our Lord and by your example of purity, I implore you to use your powerful intercession to obtain for me the virtues of trust, integrity, and simplicity in my life. I am confident that your prayers for my benefit will be heard by our Lord, Holiest of Holies. Amen.

BLESSED ARE THEY WHICH DO HUNGER AND THIRST AFTER
RIGHTEOUSNESS: FOR THEY SHALL BE FILLED. BLESSED ARE THE
MERCIFUL: FOR THEY SHALL OBTAIN MERCY.

— MATTHEW 5:6-7

SAINT CATHERINE OF GENOA

Few marriages today can survive the betrayal of an unfaithful partner no longer committed to the relationship. Many such marriages collapse, and the couples go their separate ways, often bearing emotional scars. Yet some are saved through open and honest dialogue, respect, love (if there's any to be felt underneath all the anger and hurt), and the shared goal of trying to understand what went wrong.

How difficult it is not to wear the mask of suffering and to still do good in the world when, at home, in private, your world is falling apart. Saint Catherine of Genoa suffered just such a fate, and yet, through the grace of God, she found the strength to live an honorable and purposeful life serving others. Her wayward husband finally found inspiration in her example. He dedicated himself to their marital partnership and helped her do charitable works for the rest of his life. As for Catherine, she achieved perhaps the highest measure of divine love a human might ever experience while still upon the Earth. She wrote of life, "We should not wish for anything but what comes to us from moment to moment, exercising ourselves nonetheless for good." (Ghezzi, 2000)

Lived—A.D. 1447–1510
Beatified—1737; named a saint in the Roman Martyrology by Pope Benedict XIV
Feast day—September 15
Patron saint of Genoa and Italian hospitals

Born into a well-to-do family in 1447, Caterinetta, or Catherine, was the fifth of five children. From her earliest teen years, Catherine wanted to become a nun and revealed as much to her confessor. He put her off because of her youth. Shortly thereafter, her father passed away. When she was 16, Catherine was married in an arranged match made to best serve the interests of the two families involved, but certainly not Catherine's best interests. In character and temperament, Catherine and her husband were worlds apart. She was beautiful, kind, sensible, intelligent, and deeply religious, while Julian was hot-tempered, undisciplined, and self-indulgent. He was recklessly extravagant in his spending, and his adulterous relationship with a mistress produced a child.

With no options, Catherine must have felt imprisoned in the crucible that was her marriage. From 1463 onward, Catherine battled a debilitating depression. She spent much of her time caring for the sick and the poor. When alone, she dove deeply into spiritual contemplation.

She decided on the eve of the feast of Saint Benedict in 1473 to pray to the saint for intercessory prayers, asking God to make her sick for three months so that she would be confined to bed. Within 48 hours, while kneeling for a blessing by a chaplain, she experienced a vision of our Lord carrying his cross. A torrent of love washed over her. She cried out that she was ready to declare her sins publicly if need be. After that, Catherine recorded her thoughts about her own personal defects and lack of purity before God in her *Spiritual Dialogue*, a treatise of exchanges between the body and the soul.

That year brought about her husband's bankruptcy. In due course, Julian converted and began to practice the faith. The couple decided to remain celibate from that point on. They moved out of their palatial home to a small residence near the hospital of Pammantone and, in time, literally moved into the hospital where Catherine served as administrator.

She worked tirelessly caring for the sick in both the hospital and the slums. She also did the accounting and bookwork for the hospital and engaged in intense spiritual practices that included her own fasts as well as those of the church.

In 1493, while nursing patients, Catherine caught the plague and nearly died. Then, in 1497, Julian, who'd since become a Franciscan tertiary, died, leaving Catherine a widow. Saint Catherine, who had forgiven her husband for his transgressions, used what little money he left to care for his mistress and daughter.

The end for Catherine was drawing near as well.

After a protracted illness and months of agony, she suffered a high fever and delirium and died on September 15, 1510. ✣

I see these things clearly, but words fail to describe them as I wish. What I have described is going on within my spirit, and therefore I have said it. The prison which detains me is the world; my chains, the body; the soul, illuminated by grace, comprehends how great a misery it is to be hindered from her final end, and she suffers greatly because she is very tender. She receives from God, by his grace, a certain dignity which assimilates her to him, nay, which makes her one with him by the participation of his goodness. And as it is impossible for God to suffer any pain, it is so also with those happy souls who are drawing nearer to Him. The more closely they approach Him, the more fully do they share in his perfection.

—SAINT CATHERINE OF GENOA
(CHRISTIAN CLASSICS ETHEREAL LIBRARY)

WAYS TO HONOR AND INVOKE THE BLESSINGS OF SAINT CATHERINE OF GENOA

✣ Volunteer at your local hospital or nursing home for an hour or more each week.

✣ Offer to answer phones for a domestic abuse, rape crisis, or suicide hotline.

✣ Clean out the closets and cupboards and make a contribution to local shelters for the homeless or for battered women and children.

✣ Share the wealth. Instead of eating out on the weekend or buying that latte on the way to work, one day a week save the money and put it into a jar for the needy.

✣ Make a mixed-media collage from cut-out magazine art, lines of written prayers, religious iconographic patterns, and symbols of faith to depict what you think the soul would say to the body about carnal pleasure, spiritual devotion, infidelity, and the sacrament of marriage.

✣ Isolate and study a passage from Saint Catherine of Genoa's *Spiritual Dialogue*. Use it as departure point for contemplation. She was considered a great mystic, and deep contemplation was a regular part of her sacred spiritual practice.

Prayer to Saint Catherine of Genoa

O Saint Catherine, you who turned your suffering to an intense love for God and a commitment to do good works for fellow human beings, we celebrate your strength, steadfastness of vision, and mercy for those suffering from sickness, sin, and sadness.

Protect us against depression and lift our hearts for us to our Lord that he may show mercy and compassion upon us. We venerate your spiritual effort and accomplishments and ask that you intercede on our behalf to carry our prayers and petitions before the throne of God. Inspire us to overcome the adversity in our lives and show us how to transform it into a most sacred mystical union with our Lord. Amen.

OPEN THOU MINE EYES, THAT I MAY BEHOLD WONDROUS
THINGS OUT OF THY LAW.

— PSALM 119:18

SAINT CATHERINE OF SIENA

It takes courage to speak up when you see civil or religious abuses that are a detriment to your church, community, or society at large. Without ordinary citizens becoming advocates for reform, change for the better might never happen.

Catherine of Siena was such a reformer. She bravely pointed out abuses of power and weakness of will among the clergy whenever she could. As expected, this brought down upon her the wrath of critics who suggested that she was following her will and not God's. These critics even attempted to murder her, but Catherine remained undeterred. Her goal wasn't to divide the church but to unify it through total love of God.

Caterina di Giacomo di Benincasa's was the next to the last birth in a family of 25 children. Her father, Giacomo Benincasa, was a dyer by trade. At an early age, Catherine made the decision to devote her life to God. Her parents opposed her wishes, desiring instead that she marry. But Catherine remained resolute and resisted all attempts to change her mind. She made her point to her family by cutting off her long, blond hair. Eventually, she became a member of the Dominican Third Order. She spent years in solitude, fasting, performing penance, and offering prayers until she experienced a mystical union with Christ. After that, she felt called to help others. Her first steps outward into society came when she cared for sick people in hospitals.

In 1370, the country was hit by a famine, and in 1374 the plague came. A Dominican prior named Raymond Capua, who was infected with the plague but survived, revealed that he was cured through Catherine's intercessory prayers. He later became her confident and spiritual adviser.

In time, a group of disciples began to accompany Catherine on her journeys to tend to the sick and to preach. They included both men and women, some of them Augustinians and others Dominicans. Catherine sounded a call for reform through repentance and renewal. Her success at conversion was remarkable. To accommodate all who wished to heed her call to repent and confess their sins, more confessors had to join her group of followers on missions to spread the word.

Several miracles were attributed to Catherine, including the rescinding of her mother Lapa's death. Thanks to Catherine's prayers asking God to restore her mother, Lapa was reprieved and lived to be almost 90.

Lived–A.D. 1347–1380
Canonized–1461
Feast day–April 29 (since 1969, formerly April 30)
Special titles–Doctor of the Church (conferred in 1970)
Patron saint of all of Europe (along with co-patron Saint Bridget of Sweden), Italy (along with co-patron Saint Francis of Assisi), nurses, fire protection, and activism

Catherine, five years before her own death, went to the church of Santa Cristina in the city of Pisa. She knelt before the crucifix in the church and experienced the stigmata (bleeding from her hands, as Christ's did). That the stigmata were visible to only Catherine later led to squabbles over the veracity of the event. Catherine would not live to see Pope Sixtus IV ban images showing her stigmata nor Pope Urban VIII (200 years later) lift the ban so long as the stigmata were not shown oozing blood.

In 1376, Catherine had meetings with Pope Gregory XI in Avignon (the papacy had been located there since 1309) to encourage him to return to Rome. When he died in 1378, Urban VI was elected pope in Rome while another was elected pope in Avignon. Catherine urged European leaders to recognize Urban as the legitimate pope. He sent for her, and she journeyed to Rome to work ceaselessly on his behalf.

In April 1380, Catherine suffered a stroke and died little more than a week later, but not before the stigmata appeared for everyone to see. Pope Pius II canonized her in 1461. Among her great works, she is credited with returning the papacy to Rome.

It should be noted that she never learned to read or write, but dictated more than 383 letters and a compilation of her ideas and mystical experiences known as her *Dialogue*. Catherine was declared a Doctor of the Church in 1970 (she is one of only three women ever to receive such recognition). Her body today is kept in Santa Maria sopra Minerva in Rome. Since removing the body parts, or relics, of saints for redistribution to holy places associated with that saint was the practice in the Middle Ages, her head was removed and sent to San Domenico in Siena. ✙

Thus in all things created, in all rational creatures, and in the devils is seen the glory and praise of My Name. Who can see it? The soul who is denuded of the body and has reached Me, her End, sees it clearly, and, in seeing, knows the truth. Seeing Me, the Eternal Father, she loves, and loving, she is satisfied. Satisfied, she knows the Truth, and her will is stayed in My Will, bound and made stable, so that in nothing can it suffer pain, because it has that which it desired to have, before the soul saw Me, namely, the glory and praise of My Name. She now in truth, sees it completely in My saints, in the blessed spirits, and in all creatures and things, even in the devils, as I told thee.

—SAINT CATHERINE OF SIENA
(THOROLD, 1974)

WAYS TO HONOR AND INVOKE THE BLESSINGS OF SAINT CATHERINE OF SIENA

✛ Plant some lily bulbs in your garden in honor of this great mystic, worker for the people, and spiritual reformer. Lilies have long been Saint Catherine's emblem. When summer comes and your lilies bloom, put them on your altar.

✛ Read *The Dialogue*, translated by Suzanne Nofke (Paulist Press, 1980), and reflect on the thoughts and mystical insights of Saint Catherine.

✛ Take a stand on an issue for which you believe that reform is needed for the good of all. Let your voice be heard. Participate according to your ability and schedule. Can you play a role in a telephone tree, a letter-writing campaign, the door-to-door distribution of flyers, or informal community meetings? Ask God for his blessing on your work and give all glory and recognition back to him.

Novena to Saint Catherine of Siena

Heavenly Father, your glory is in your saints. We praise your glory in the life of the admirable Saint Catherine of Siena, virgin and doctor of the church. Her whole life was a noble sacrifice inspired by an ardent love of Jesus, your unblemished lamb. In troubled times she strenuously upheld the rights of his beloved spouse, the church. Father, honor her merits and hear her prayers for each of us, and for our whole parish family dedicated to her. Help us to pass unscathed through the corruption of this world, and to remain unmistakably faithful to the church in word, deed, and example. Help us always to see in the Vicar of Christ an anchor in the storms of life and a beacon of light to the harbor of your love, in this dark night of your times and men's souls. We ask this through Jesus, your Son, in the bond of the Holy Spirit. Amen.

(Pause to pray for your own intentions.)

Saint Catherine of Siena, pray for us.

Recite this novena nine times in a row for nine days in a row.

— CALAMARI AND DIPASQUA, 1999

GOD IS A SPIRIT: AND THEY THAT WORSHIP HIM, MUST WORSHIP
HIM IN SPIRIT AND IN TRUTH.

— JOHN 4:24

SAINT CLARE OF ASSISI

implicity of life means a life unencumbered. But its relevance goes far beyond having few tangible possessions. It may also mean a spare quality of mind—getting rid of the myriad thoughts that invade our minds and distract us from a single focus or purpose. Mindless self-talk goes on endlessly whether or not we are aware of it. Most of us carry around so much emotional baggage that psychologists have likened it to a broken record or a tape replaying over and over.

Perhaps the saints realized that to develop that razor sharp focus on God, they needed to bring about both an outer and an inner release of "stuff." This includes shutting down the senses in order to forget about the body long enough to allow the mind to dive deeply into prayer, contemplation, and meditation, with the goal nothing less than a mystical union with Christ and thereby with all things. Freeing yourself of possessions is another way to emulate Christ's teaching and way of life.

Clare, a medieval contemplative, chose such a life. She embraced simplicity in an austere form of holy poverty. She shunned shoes, sandals, and stockings.

She and her nuns were vegetarians, slept on the hard ground, and never spoke except when performing their charitable works. They lived entirely on alms and renounced communal possessions. Clare wore a hair shirt next to her skin, and during Lent she ate only bread and water. She would not ask another to do what she herself was not willing to do. Each morning, it was Clare who lit the candles and rang the choir bells.

Love him totally who gave himself totally for your love.

—SAINT CLARE (THIGPEN, 2001)

Saint Clare was born in Assisi into the noble family of Offreduccio. By the time she reached puberty, her family had already chosen a man for her to marry, but Clare would not hear of it. She preferred to listen to sermons by a certain Saint Francis of Assisi. When she was 18, her heart and mind were so touched by the Lenten Sermons of Francis in the church of Giorgio that she decided to renounce her life and become a nun. Her decision was not well received by her family, but Clare would not succumb to their attempts to change her mind.

Lived—A.D. 1193–1253
Feast day—August 11 (formerly August 12)
Patron saint of television and television writers, embroiderers, good weather, sufferers of eye diseases, and women in childbirth

One Palm Sunday in 1212, Clare went to the Cathedral of Assisi for the blessings of palms. Too shy to go up to the altar rail to receive her branch of olive, she remained in place until the bishop approached and handed her the branch. That night, she stole away from her home and walked about a mile to where Saint Francis and his followers were staying. She met him at the chapel of our Lady of the Angels. There, Saint Francis cut off her hair, and she put on his habit, a sackcloth tied with cord. He arranged for her to go to the Benedictine convent of Saint Paul.

Her family and friends made every effort to draw her out and away from the religious life, but they did not succeed. Later Saint Francis moved Clare to a different nunnery, eventually placing her in the little house contiguous to San Damiano, the church he had restored. In 1215, he named her founder and abbess of the new order of Poor Clares, or Minoresses, and he wrote a simple rule for them to follow.

Although initially reluctant to serve in that leadership capacity, Clare nevertheless served as abbess for the next 40 years. During that time, she welcomed into her community her two sisters and her mother. She eventually wrote a rule for other women, and it became the first rule for governing a convent that was ever written by a woman.

For years, the Poor Clares practiced their faith and a simple life of austerity. But after some time, Francis convinced Clare to sleep on a mattress and eat a little bread every day. Eventually, Clare advocated a more moderate approach to her order's way of life, suggesting that the women offer reasonable service to Christ and a sacrifice tempered by prudence.

Clare suffered terribly over the 27 or so years after Saint Francis's death in 1226. During those years, she sewed altar cloths and said special prayers for the town of Assisi whenever the community was in the throes of a crisis. Many church leaders visited her, including popes and cardinals. Clare died in 1253 and was canonized two years later by Pope Alexander IV. After being buried in the church of San Giorgio, her body was later transferred to Santa Chiara in Assisi.

The Poor Clares struggled with the poverty issue until their stance was reformed by Colette in the fifteenth century. Saint Clare herself never left the Assisi convent during her life, but the order she founded gained popularity and expanded outward across Europe. Today, unfortunately, there are far fewer Poor Clare convents than there once were. ✠

WAYS TO HONOR AND INVOKE THE BLESSINGS OF SAINT CLARE

✢ Spend time with nature. Try to feel the connections among all things as experienced by Saint Clare and Saint Francis.

✢ Sew an altar cloth.

✢ Make your backyard a wildlife sanctuary with food, water, and nesting materials for birds and squirrels.

✢ Create a sacred space in your home where you can practice contemplation in total silence.

AFFIRMATION

The enchantment of the material world is giving way to an intense love of the spiritual world. I vow to spend more minutes each day in the temple of my own heart where I shall be like a flower, opening myself to the Lord.

POEM FROM THE GIRL WHO OFFERED HERSELF TO THE LORD

What care I for the things of this world?
Silks and pearls and leather shoes,
They have no claim on me.
My soul's ensnared by a lover bee
Who drops pollen in my heart
To set me free.
I, Clare, say, "Lord, I am yours. Take my life.
It is hardly mine."

Prayer to Saint Clare

O Saint Clare, who turned from the temptations of this world to embrace a life of holy poverty dedicated to God, we celebrate your single-minded devotion and purity. Mercifully pray with us and for us to our Lord, asking for strength of purpose and focus of vision on our needy brothers and sisters and also the animals of the field and sky. Obtain for us the grace to renounce worldly goods and to acquire the strength to fight against the twin temptations of gluttony and selfishness. Saint Clare, your life on earth served as a mirror of purity and love for our Lord. May we find inspiration in your example so that we never cease striving for the riches in heaven rather than those on Earth. Amen.

WALK IN WISDOM TOWARD THEM THAT ARE WITHOUT . . .

— COLOSSIANS 4:5

SAINT DYMPHNA

Those who suffer depression or other mental maladies or who care for loved ones so afflicted know how indifferent society can often be. In some parts of the world, the mentally ill are still treated like pariahs. Yet thanks to the work of advocates for the mentally ill, this health issue is no longer relegated to the proverbial closet. Today, most professionals realize that mental illness affects not only the individual but the entire family, and they know how devastating the disease can be for the sufferer. Saint Dymphna also would know these truths only too well.

She was born in Ireland to a powerful pagan chieftain and a Christian mother who was both devout and beautiful. Dymphna was taught Christian beliefs. When the girl turned 14, her mother passed away. Dymphna's father was stricken with grief and lapsed into a state of mental illness. Longing for someone to share his life and his bed, he turned all of his attention to finding another mate. He dispatched scouts throughout the land in hopes of locating a new woman.

His instructions were simple: the woman had to look like his previous wife and also be of noble birth. This turned out to be an impossible task.

Whether it was his advisors who gave him the idea of marrying his own daughter or his own crazed mental instability that guided him is unclear. In any case, he focused his obsession on the now 15-year-old Dymphna and, possibly, made her a victim of sexual abuse.

The girl fled as far as Belgium with her confessor, Saint Gerebran, and a couple of friends. There they lived like hermits, but it wasn't long until her father found her. Immediately, he issued an order to behead the priest. He then demanded that Dymphna return to the land of her birth and be with him. When she refused, he cut off her head with his sword.

Lived—A.D. 605–620
Martyred—Virgin martyr
Feast day—May 15
Patron saint of the mentally ill, sleepwalkers, incest victims, runaways, and epileptics

Dymphna was buried where she fell, in Gheel, Belgium, some 25 miles from Antwerp. At her shrine, many miracles have reportedly taken place, including cures for those suffering from insanity or epilepsy. One legend says that five mentally ill people fell asleep at her shrine and were instantly healed. The shrine became such a popular pilgrimage site that in the thirteenth century a hospital was built near the tomb. Today, Gheel is in the forefront of seeking innovative ways to treat mental illness. ✛

…I am the root and the offspring of David, and the bright and morning star.

—REVELATIONS 22:16

WAYS TO HONOR AND INVOKE THE BLESSINGS OF SAINT DYMPHNA

✛ Expand your understanding of diseases such as depression, schizophrenia, bipolar disorder, obsessive-compulsive disorder, phobias, and the like. Look for information at www.mentalhealth.org (U.S. Department of Health and Human Services), www.nmha.org (National Mental Health Association), and www.mentalhealth.org.uk (the largest mental health site in the United Kingdom).

✛ If you or someone you know is the victim of sexual abuse, seek out someone you trust to confide in—a family member, school counselor, rape crisis center worker, doctor, or friend. Let them help you protect yourself while you find the best-qualified professional help available.

✛ Make a contribution of time or money (or both) to a teen shelter for runaways, or, if your church doesn't already have a program or a center for teens to help them deal with their problems in a faith-focused way, volunteer to spearhead a committee to establish one.

✛ If you or someone you love suffers from mental illness or sexual abuse, take a class in art therapy, dream work, and/or meditation to develop tools that can help with healing and wholeness.

✛ Ask Saint Dymphna for her intercessory prayers for protection and help.

✛ Put on some soft Celtic music. Lie flat on the floor and gently tense and relax each part of your body, starting at your feet and working your way to your neck and head. Breathe in and out several times to cleanse your body of any lingering tension. Close your eyes and imagine you are in a picturesque country setting (like Saint Dymphna's homeland of Ireland). Put in all the things that would make this scene natural and beautiful, including animals, rocks, trees, water, sky, and flowers. See a bee flying upward from a flower. See it disappear into the sky where a bird circles high above. Follow the bird as it lifts higher and higher. Watch it until you can see it become a speck and disappear. Let your mind soar higher still. Think of the endlessness of space, the great expanse of eternity. Imagine this as the place where God and saintly luminaries dwell, and you too are there.

✛ Sit for 10 minutes (set an egg timer, if you must) and allow your mind to wrap itself around the following question: How may I cultivate the qualities Jesus most loved in his disciples—innocence, purity of thought, faith, love, self-control, self-discipline, devotion, and wisdom?

AFFIRMATIONS

My inner landscape holds a special, sacred place. When emotional storms rage, I retreat to this safe place where I abide in peace.

God is watching over me and protecting me, now and always.

POEM FROM SAINT DYMPHNA TO HER HOLY FATHER

Oh father, how I long to flee
This world of shameful deeds,
To hide from those who would do me wrong,
Lose myself in the glory of thee.
I long to drink from thy wisdom well
And see with sacred sight.
I yearn to gaze at thy blessed face
And drown in beams of thy holy light.

Prayer to Saint Dymphna

O God, you gave Saint Dymphna to your church as a model of all virtues, especially holy purity, and willed that she should seal her faith with her innocent blood and perform numerous miracles. Grant that we who honor her as patroness of those afflicted with nervous and mental illness may continue to enjoy her powerful intercession and protection and attain eternal life. We ask this in the name of Jesus Christ our Lord. Amen.

WE MUST PRAY LITERALLY WITHOUT CEASING—WITHOUT CEASING: IN
EVERY OCCURRENCE AND EMPLOYMENT OF OUR LIVES. YOU KNOW I
MEAN THAT PRAYER OF THE HEART WHICH IS INDEPENDENT OF PLACE OR
SITUATION, OR WHICH IS, RATHER, A HABIT OF LIFTING UP THE HEART
TO GOD, AS IN A CONSTANT COMMUNICATION WITH HIM.
— SAINT ELIZABETH ANN SETON (THIGPEN, 2001)

SAINT ELIZABETH ANN SETON

None of us really knows what's ahead in life. No matter how well we plan and prepare, the winds of fortune can shift in an instant. One day you have wealth, and the next you lose it all. Imagine battling poverty, the death of your spouse, and the challenge of feeding and raising five children by yourself. Then, when you at last find a glimmer of hope in the act of embracing a new faith, your family and friends turn against you.

Saint Elizabeth Ann Seton lived through this very experience. She exemplifies how a woman in eighteenth century America, with all the social mores and economic restrictions that defined her gender and her choices, could survive to discover a new life and a faith that she likely never envisioned while she was growing up.

Born in New York City into a wealthy Anglican family, Elizabeth's future seemed secure. Her father was a doctor and professor of anatomy at what is now Columbia University. Although her mother died when Elizabeth was three, her father continued to raise her in the genteel and elite society of New York City.

She met wealthy merchant William Magee Seton when she was 19. William and Elizabeth married in 1794 and had five children, two sons and three daughters. Elizabeth was active in charity work, establishing the Society for the Relief of Poor Widows and Children in 1797. When William's father died in 1798, however, the family business slipped into a steep decline and soon went bankrupt. William and Elizabeth had been married only nine years. William also had several siblings of his own for whom he was responsible. To make matters even worse, he contracted tuberculosis.

In search of a warmer climate and hoping for a cure, William journeyed with Elizabeth and Anna Marie (their oldest daughter) to Italy in 1803. The other children stayed behind with relatives. Shortly after making the voyage, William died just two days after Christmas, leaving Elizabeth a poor widow with five fatherless children.

Elizabeth now had to deal with Italian law. She buried her husband as quickly as she could, but by the time she was ready to return to New York, Anna Marie had contracted scarlet fever. Elizabeth wrote to a friend that she thought she might go crazy if she weren't able to think of God constantly, in every moment. Just the thought of God, she said, pulled her into stillness and peace.

Lived–A.D. 1775–1821
Beatified–1963
Canonized–1975
Feast day–January 4
Patron saint of persons rejected for their Catholic faith, of dying children, and of those who have lost parents

Through the generosity of two Italian Catholic families, Elizabeth and Anna Marie stayed on in Italy for another year. Spiritually inspired by Catholicism, Elizabeth converted two years later on March 14, 1805.

The conversion fulfilled her spiritually but alienated her family. With little or no financial assistance from relatives, Elizabeth looked for other options. For a time, she rented out rooms to boarders. Then, acting on a suggestion by a priest, Elizabeth opened a girls' school in Baltimore in June 1808. It didn't take long for Elizabeth to draw around her a community of women who shared her thinking and beliefs.

On March 25, 1809, Elizabeth and four companions founded another school, this one for poor children, and also formed a religious community, the Sisters of Saint Joseph. The women took vows of obedience, chastity, and poverty.

At the beginning of summer that same year, Elizabeth and her sister nuns took over the rule of the Daughters of Charity of Saint Vincent de Paul in Emmitsburg, Maryland, a step approved of by the bishop of Baltimore, James Carroll. Elizabeth was elected Mother Superior and was now caring for this new order as well as her own children, whether the children were at the convent or staying elsewhere— the boys attending a Catholic boy's school and the girls living at their mother's boarding schools.

In 1812, the community of nuns became officially known as the Daughters of Charity of Saint Joseph. Elizabeth served as superior. The nuns, now numbering 18, started many orphanages and hospitals under Mother Seton's leadership and also established the excellent Catholic parochial school system in the United States.

But Elizabeth was to suffer yet another blow in 1816 when her youngest daughter Rebecca died. Saddened, but not broken in spirit, she turned once again to God for comfort. Then Anna Marie died from a protracted illness, and her death delivered a crushing blow to Saint Elizabeth. In a letter to a friend she wrote:

The separation from my angel has left so new and deep an impression on my mind, that if I was not obliged to live in these dear ones I should unconsciously die in her.

—ELIZABETH ANN SETON (REJNIS, 2001)

By the time Elizabeth died on January 4, 1821, the Daughters of Charity of Saint Joseph had expanded to 20 communities throughout America. Three miracles were ascribed to her intercession, including two cases of a miraculous healing of meningitis and one of leukemia. Pope John Paul XXIII beatified her in 1963, and Pope Paul VI canonized her in 1975, making her the first native-born American saint. Her body lies under an altar in the chapel of the National Shrine of Saint Elizabeth Seton in Emmitsburg, Maryland.

Mother Elizabeth Seton's story inspires everyone, but perhaps most especially those who feel the kind of grief-stricken desperation and nihilism that can come with crushing loss. As her own life shows us, the most healing balm to be had is the one that comes though prayer, faith, and devotion to our beloved comforter. ✝

WAYS TO HONOR AND INVOKE THE BLESSINGS OF SAINT ELIZABETH ANN SETON

✝ Visit the National Shrine of Saint Elizabeth Ann Seton as well as the Stone House in Emmitsburg, Maryland, where Mother Seton and her companions first lived in 1809. For information on the museum and the nearby Grotto of Lourdes, go to www.setonshrine.org.

✝ Explore becoming a volunteer at a hospice to give comfort, support, and love to those who are making the transit from life to death.

✝ Read *Elizabeth Bayley Seton, 1774–1821*, by Annabelle M. Melville (Pillar Books, 1985) and other books about Mother Seton.

✝ Turn off the phone, television, radio, and lights. Sit in a comfortable chair. Place a shawl or throw over your lap if you think you will get cold. It's important to feel safe and warm. Think about how you can turn off your physical senses (just as you did the phone, lights, etc.). Breathe deeply, and mentally create a sacred space in your heart. Think of all the losses that Saint Elizabeth Ann Seton experienced in her life. Now consider how you might feel if God started subtracting people and things from your life. Would you still love him? What might God be teaching us by allowing us to experience such losses and reversals of fortune? Finish this meditation by feeling the holy presence. Allow yourself to feel the warmth of his light filling you. In this expanded state of consciousness, consider how all peoples of the world could be connected by the invisible rays of God's love.

AFFIRMATIONS

I will think of God constantly in every moment, as Saint Elizabeth Ann Seton did.

I will seek God's blessing on every choice I make, every action I take.

I choose happiness over sadness, hope over despair, peace over stress, and humility over vanity.

✝✝✝✝✝✝✝✝✝✝✝✝✝✝✝✝✝✝✝✝✝✝✝✝✝

Prayer to Saint Elizabeth Ann Seton

O Saint Elizabeth Ann Seton, you suffered innumerable losses during your lifetime yet remained fervently devoted to our Lord Jesus Christ and faithfully carried on the work of the church, his sacred spouse on Earth. Inspire us to follow your example of deepening our love and commitment to God in the face of our adversities and reversals of fortune. Amen.

✝✝✝✝✝✝✝✝✝✝✝✝✝✝✝✝✝✝✝✝✝✝✝✝✝

BUT JESUS SAID, SUFFER LITTLE CHILDREN, AND FORBID THEM NOT,
TO COME UNTO ME: FOR OF SUCH IS THE KINGDOM OF HEAVEN.

— MATTHEW 19:14

SAINT FRANCES XAVIER CABRINI

Children who have been orphaned or injured by the ravages of war or by abuse have needs that go beyond housing, clothing, and food. Their road to healing and wholeness requires a great deal more—love, patience, understanding, and spiritual and educational resources to prepare them for life. These are qualities that some people seem born with while others learn them as they rear children themselves. As a child from a large family, herself an orphan, it is likely that Saint Frances Xavier Cabrini instinctively knew what children needed to succeed in life. And she made that her life's work.

The youngest of 13 children, Maria Francesca Cabrini was born in 1850 near Pavia, Italy. When she reached 20 years of age, both her parents died. Heeding an inner urge to become a nun, Frances first thought of where she'd been educated and then applied there. Voicing concerns about her health, that convent, as well as a second one she hoped to enter, turned her away. Young Frances then decided to teach school and, about the same time, to take a private vow of virginity.

When a parish priest asked her to go to Lombardy to reorganize an orphanage that had been badly mismanaged by its previous overseer and founder, Frances eagerly accepted. Eventually, however, the bishop closed down that orphanage and suggested that Frances take up missionary work.

By now she had seven companions who had joined her in Lombardy. Together they established a foundation at Grumello in Milan in 1880 and also in Rome in 1887. Papal approval was soon given for her Missionary Sisters of the Sacred Heart. While she expressed interest in following in the footsteps of her namesake, Saint Francis Xavier, and going to China and parts of Asia, church leaders had other ideas. They thought she'd be perfect to minister to the large population of Italian immigrants in America.

Frances made the trip to New York to visit the city's poverty-stricken Italian immigrant neighborhoods. There were plenty of children to teach, but no school or orphanage. Archbishop Michael Corrigan told her to go back to Italy, a suggestion Frances did not accept. Instead, she mentioned her papers from the pope, and she stayed in New York. In 1890, she not only established an orphanage but also moved to the area known as West Park on the Hudson River. There she built a novitiate and a house for her congregation.

Lived–A.D. 1850–1917
Canonized–1946
Feast day–November 13 (some sources cite December 22)
Patron saint of immigrants, emigrants, and hospital administrators

Local merchants made things a little easier for Mother Cabrini with generous donations that allowed her to feed and care for the poor. In time, her foundations expanded and were established in major American cities, including New York, Chicago, and New Orleans, and in such countries as Nicaragua and England.

The care, feeding, and education of orphans remained a lifelong calling, leading Mother Cabrini to establish institutions like summer camps for orphans, including one in Golden, Colorado. She also worked tirelessly to introduce new hospitals into various cities of the United States. Before her death, she founded more than 50 charitable centers. She was a woman who would climb mountains, crawl into caves, visit slums, and venture into South American jungles—whatever it took to fulfill her promise to help those in need.

The year 1907 was significant for Mother Cabrini for two reasons: it was the year her order's rule was approved and the year she received her U.S. citizenship. She was the first U.S. citizen to arrive on American shores as an immigrant and ultimately be canonized.

After going on a six-month retreat in 1916, Frances Xavier Cabrini contracted malaria and died in Chicago on December 22, 1917. Pope Pius XII canonized her in 1946. Today her body lies asleep in the Lord at New York's Mother Cabrini High School. ☩

I travel, work, suffer my weak health, meet with a thousand difficulties, but all these are nothing, for this world is so small. To me, space is an imperceptible object, as I am accustomed to dwell in eternity.

—SAINT FRANCES XAVIER CABRINI
(THIGPEN, 2001)

WAYS TO HONOR AND INVOKE THE BLESSINGS OF SAINT FRANCES XAVIER CABRINI

☩ Use your creativity to set up an oral history project for one of the senior centers in the Italian-American community of your town or city. Ask those Catholic seniors who are immigrants or first-generation children of immigrant parents to share their life stories. Be sure to focus on how they got through the tough times. What might their own spiritual message be for the offspring of other immigrants? Who were their favorite saints? In what ways might Mother Cabrini have connected with their lives? Perhaps the senior center can keep these oral histories on a web page or videotape them and maintain a library of them for your community.

✛ Set aside time each day to de-stress body and mind. Then pray and meditate on Mother Cabrini's words: "Space is an imperceptible object, as I am accustomed to dwell in eternity."

✛ Find out from your church if there are needy families or children who live with a single working parent. Make five hot meals that can be frozen in plastic containers and given to the family so they'll have a frozen homemade entrée for every day of the workweek.

✛ Make some Italian cookies. Put them in a pretty box adorned with images of Mother Cabrini and give them to a nursing home or senior center for Italian-Americans, a children's shelter, or the poor.

✛ Dive deeply inward. Listen intently. Be present. Expect the unexpected. Allow God's blessing to hold you, fill you, and radiate outward from you into the world.

✛ Be still—physically and mentally. Try to recapture the feeling of the child within you. Pray for all children on Earth.

AFFIRMATIONS

I will try emulating Saint Frances Xavier Cabrini's example of love and support for all children.

I will replace emotional outbursts with calm civility, anger with patience, displeasure with love, and fearfulness with hope and understanding.

Prayer to Saint Frances Xavier Cabrini

O Blessed Mother Cabrini, who was sent to America to minister to immigrants from your motherland, we pay homage to you for a lifetime of hard work caring for the Lord's hungry, orphaned, and displaced children. Pray for us that we may perform our life's work in ways that may be holy and pleasing to God and glorify his precious name. May we also be able to bring children to the Lord and guide them toward a strong spiritual life in him that they may see God as an anchor and pole star to guide them throughout their lives. Amen.

BLESSED ARE THE PURE IN HEART FOR THEY SHALL SEE GOD.
BLESSED ARE THE PEACE-MAKERS: FOR THEY SHALL BE CALLED THE
CHILDREN OF GOD. BLESSED ARE THEY WHICH ARE PERSECUTED
FOR RIGHTEOUSNESS' SAKE: FOR THEIRS IS THE KINGDOM OF HEAVEN.

— MATTHEW 5:8–10

SAINT FRANCIS OF ASSISI

Some receive the call to serve God in early childhood, others later in life, and still others never hear or heed the call. When that call comes as an inner urge or inspirational thought guiding us toward a certain action, we do not necessarily have to abandon our worldly duties to our families and our communities and suddenly enter a religious order—indeed that path isn't for everyone.

There are a myriad of ways to do God's work, and in some situations, that might just be by living our lives in an exemplary way for others to witness. For Saint Francis, the sacrifices were great; he suffered abject poverty, but the goal for him was nothing less than to merge every fiber of his being into a oneness with the crucified Christ!

Born into a wealthy Italian family in 1181, Francesco Bernadone was christened John, but Francesco (or "the Frenchman") was the affectionate name his mother gave him because his father was away on business in France when baby Francesco was born. His father, an Italian merchant, did considerable trading with businesses in France. Francis, a dutiful son, helped his father run the business.

Lived–A.D. 1181–1226
Canonized–1228
Feast day–October 4
Impression of the Stigmata–September 17
Special titles–Seraphic Father and Saint, Wonder Worker
Patron saint of Italy, ecologists, animals, tapestry makers, and merchants

Life was good until strife broke out between the towns of Assisi and Perugia. Francis was captured and imprisoned by the Perugians. During his year in captivity, he fell gravely ill. After his recovery, he vowed to fight with the forces in southern Italy. One day, outfitted in new clothes and weaponry, he met a poor fellow with nothing but the tattered clothes on his back. Francis wasted no time exchanging clothes with the man before continuing on his way to Spoleto. Once again he fell ill. He perceived a voice telling him to turn back and "serve the master, not the man."

So Francis returned home to the life he'd always known. Then one day, while out riding, he came upon a leper. He was so touched by the man's sores and obvious physical suffering that he kissed the man and gave him alms. From that time forward, Francis began serving the poor and the sick, helping them however he could.

Once, while praying at a dilapidated church known as San Damiano of Assisi, Francis perceived a message coming from a Byzantine-style cross. It urged him to repair the church. Francis wasted no time selling bolts of his father's cloth to buy building supplies. He took the money to a priest of San Damiano, asking him to accept the money and to let Francis stay with him. The priest refused the former but accepted the latter.

When Francis's father found out what he had done, he was furious. He went in search of Francis, dragged him home, beat him severely, and locked him away. Pica, Francis's mother, released him, and Francis returned to San Damiano, where his father again found him and demanded that he return the money and come home—or renounce his inheritance. Francis refused and was shortly thereafter summoned to appear before the Bishop of Assisi, who also told Francis to give back the money.

Francis began removing every piece of his clothing, telling the Bishop that his father owned them as well. This was a pivotal moment in Francis's life, one from which there was no turning back. As Joseph Campbell, the late mythologist, would have pointed out, Francis had accepted the call to adventure.

Francis rebuilt San Damiano using monies begged from the townspeople. He chose to live life as a penniless pilgrim, serving the poor and infirm, including lepers, and eventually establishing a communal life with several other men near a leper colony on the outskirts of Assisi. In 1210, he wrote a primitive rule for his small order, and it received papal approval. Francis and his brethren began preaching and undertaking pilgrimages to reach a wider audience for God's words.

Francis's order, the Order of Friars Minor (or Franciscans), quickly grew to include 5,000 individuals. Francis resigned his office of Minister-General at the meeting of the General Chapter of 1220. Then, in 1221, he drew up a new rule for the order and also instructions for Tertiaries, or those who would follow Franciscan ideals but had families and lived outside the religious order.

While visiting an extremely ill Saint Clare of Assisi in 1224, he wrote his now famous *Canticle of the Sun*. In that same year, he also experienced stigmata during an ecstatic, contemplative state, and the wounds remained on his body for the rest of his life. Francis later went blind and eventually died in 1226 at the rural chapel of Portiuncula, in Assisi, the place where his collective was first formed. He was 45. He was canonized in 1228, and in 1230, his body was moved from the church of San Giorgio in Assisi to the New Basilica, built to house his remains.

In the end, Francis's "call" brought him to an all-encompassing love for God and total identification with the sufferings of Christ. ✠

All creatures have the same source as we have. Like us, they derive the life of thought, love, and will from the Creator. Not to hurt our humble brethren is our first duty to them; but to stop there is a complete misapprehension of the intentions of Providence. We have a higher mission. God wishes that we should succor them whenever they require it.

—SAINT FRANCIS OF ASSISI (THIGPEN, 2001)

WAYS TO HONOR AND INVOKE THE BLESSINGS OF SAINT FRANCIS

✠ Install in your backyard or garden, or even in a screened-in porch, a statue of Saint Francis. If your statue is outside, put up a birdfeeder and maintain it in the name of Saint Francis, who loved all creatures, perhaps especially birds.

✠ Hang the print of a beautiful painting of Saint Francis, such as the work by Italian artist Giotto titled *Saint Francis Preaching to the Birds*, in an indoor or outdoor garden room of your home.

✠ Do charitable works for the poor, especially those poor who are sick or otherwise suffering.

✠ Take your pet animals to be blessed by the priest.

✠ Read biographies of Saint Francis's life, including Julien Green's *God's Fool: The Life and Times of Francis of Assisi* (Harper and Row, 1985).

✠ Make a beautiful crucifix in pique assiette (broken china) mosaics to hang in your garden to remind you of when Saint Francis was praying before the crucifix in the church of San Damiano. Have your priest bless it.

Novena to Saint Francis

Lord, make me an instrument of your peace,
Where there is hatred, let me sow love;
Where there is injury, pardon;
Where there is doubt, faith;
Where there is despair, hope;
Where there is darkness, light;
Where there is sadness, joy.

O divine master,
Grant that I may not so much seek
To be consoled as to console,
To be understood as to understand,
To be loved as to love.

For it is in giving that we receive,
In pardoning that we are pardoned, and in
Dying that we are born to Eternal Life.
Amen.

Saint Francis of Assisi, reflection of Christ
through your life of poverty and humility,
grant us through your intercession the graces
we so much need for soul and body.
Especially during this novena, we ask for
(mention your request). We also ask your
blessings on all those whom we love.
Amen.

Recite this novena nine times in a row for nine days in a row.

—CALAMARI AND DIPASQUA, 1999

. . . HOW BEAUTIFUL ARE THE FEET OF THEM THAT PREACH THE GOSPEL
OF PEACE, AND BRING GLAD TIDINGS OF GOOD THINGS!

— ROMANS 10:14–15

SAINT FRANCIS XAVIER

ollow your bliss, mythologist Joseph Campbell advised, and doors that you didn't know existed will open for you. Some souls seem to know from their earliest childhood what they want to do and be when they grow up. For others, the choice is not so clear. God knows better than you what you are best suited to do, and if you just follow your bliss and listen to his call to your soul, your life can be both different and rewarding. For Saint Francis Xavier, it was just this sort of deep, heartfelt impulse that changed everything for him.

Francis, a Basque Spaniard, was born near Pampalona, Spain, at the castle of Navarre. He planned to become a scholar and, pursuing that goal, eventually finished his course of study at the University of Paris. While in Paris, however, his inquisitive mind and open heart drew him to Saint Ignatius of Loyola, who was just forming the Society of Jesus. In 1534, Francis took his vows at Monmartre to become one of the first seven Jesuits. In Venice, three years afterward, Francis was ordained a priest and his missionary work began.

Lived–A.D. 1506–1552
Canonized–1622
Feast day–December 3
Patron saint of foreign missions, tourists, India, Borneo, the East Indies, Australia, Pakistan, and Japan

Francis initially went to Lisbon. In 1541, he set sail for Goa despite the fact that he had problems learning foreign languages and got terribly seasick on boats. Goa, then a Portuguese colony, was located on India's southeastern coast along the Arabian Sea. The invitation from King John III of Portugal asking Francis to serve there gave Francis a mandate to evangelize the East Indies. The trip alone took 13 months. During the long journey, Francis prayed and ministered to everyone, whether they suffered ailments of a spiritual or physical nature.

For Francis, Goa would make a perfect headquarters, but there was much initial work to be done among the lax Portuguese Catholic inhabitants. Francis found that the locals were mistreating their slaves, ignoring the poor, openly engaging in illicit sex with concubines, and having children outside the sacrament of marriage. Francis focused his efforts on reform, encouraging the men to care for their offspring by the concubines, to treat their slaves humanely, and to do whatever they could for the poor. With dedication, fortitude, and spiritual vision, Francis worked hard each day: mornings were spent visiting prisons and hospitals; in the afternoons, he taught catechism to slaves and children. Sunday too was a long day, with time devoted to saying a special, separate mass for lepers.

In his work with the indigenous people, Francis focused on the poor. He lived among the poor, slept on the ground or in huts, consumed only rice and water, and sang Christian teachings and truths set to the music of popular tunes. He taught these people the Ten Commandments, the Apostle's Creed, and the Lord's Prayer. When people declared their faith, he baptized them. In this way, he tried to improve their often miserable existence and to ensure that he'd done everything he could to help them on their way when the Lord called them to their heavenly home.

Over the next seven years, Francis served the poor in southern India, Ceylon, Malacca, Malaysia, and the Molucca Islands. He was particularly successful in converting the Paravas in southern India, and some scholars have even suggested that he probably saved them from extermination. Driven by the aim of drawing as many souls to the Lord as he could in his lifetime, Francis worked tirelessly toward that goal throughout the East.

In 1549, he set off for Japan. He made some converts along the way, but his goal was to see the emperor. Francis soon discovered that because he dressed in such poor garments and was without appropriate gifts, he would not be granted an audience.

There was also a great deal of fighting going on among opposing political factions in the capital. Hoping the end justified the means, Francis found and changed into more regal attire and, as an emissary of the king of Portugal, offered the ruler a clock and a music box. In return, Francis was given an empty monastery and protection. In time, Francis converted a few thousand Japanese who, sadly, would later suffer persecution for their Christian beliefs.

Francis returned to Goa and then left for China. En route on December 3, 1552, at the island of Sancian, he fell ill and died. He was 46. His body was returned to Goa in quicklime to preserve it, and it has since remained enshrined there. His right arm was transported to the Church of the Gesù in Rome in 1615. He was canonized seven years later.

In 1927, Pope Pius XI declared Francis Xavier the patron of foreign missions. In the course of his life, he had baptized over 40,000 people throughout the regions of the East where he ministered to the poor, the disenfranchised, and the forgotten children of God. ✠

✛ Consider sponsoring a poor Indian Christian family or making a donation to a Christian orphanage in honor of the work done by Saint Francis Xavier.

✛ Make a pilgrimage to the Good Church of Jesus in Goa, India, where the relics of this saint are held, or to the Church of the Gesù in Rome, where his right arm is kept.

✛ On Saint Francis Xavier's feast day, prominently display a work of art you've created in his honor and say prayers to him. On this day, instead of feasting, consider fasting—taking only rice and water as Saint Francis Xavier did when he lived among the poor in Goa.

AFFIRMATIONS

I will see the clouds in the sky as the work of God, the divine painter. When misfortune comes into my life, I will think of God's hand painting the adversity into lessons from which my soul learns and grows.

Like Saint Francis Xavier, I will become a magnet to draw many souls to the Lord.

I will think powerful, positive thoughts in the present to counteract all the negative thinking I have done in the past.

Prayer to Saint Francis Xavier

Saint Francis Xavier, we seek your prayers of intercession to our Lord for strength, inspiration, endurance, and protection for our missionaries and their work. May the light of the missionaries' love for Jesus ever illuminate the Lord's way for them. Beloved Saint Francis, we ask you to pray with us for the Lord's love and guidance upon those who have dedicated their lives to his work. May our Lord Jesus Christ give them strength where there is weakness, love where there is disgust, and peaceful thoughts where there is a confused or troubled mind. And we pray, too, for your help—that when we share our Lord's teaching with others, that their minds might be open and receptive. Amen.

FOR YE WERE SOMETIME DARKNESS, BUT NOW ARE YE LIGHT IN THE
LORD: WALK AS CHILDREN OF LIGHT.

— EPHESIANS 5:8

SAINT GERARD MAJELLA

How can we live an inner-directed life if we never make time to go inward? The eight-hour workday seems like a myth when we still have to prepare dinner, help with homework, and do the laundry. When we finally have a moment to sit down, to turn our attention inward, do we? Or are we so tired that if we close our eyes for a second, fatigue pulls us straight into sleep? How important is it to keep that daily appointment with God?

Saint Gerard seemed to know from boyhood on. He, like so many of the saints, learned that all the work had to be done, but the most important work of the day was making time for God.

Gerard Majella was born in Muro, Lucano, approximately 50 miles from the city of Naples. His father, Dominic Majella, worked as a tailor but died when Gerard was still a young child. His mother, a pious woman, apprenticed him to a tailor, a man who loved him like a son. Gerard's supervisor, however, treated him cruelly, eventually causing the young man to leave and to find work as a servant to the bishop of Lacedogna.

The bishop was a hard man to please, but Gerard stuck it out, staying until the prelate's death. Afterwards, Gerard found other work, dividing his income between his mother and the poor. Yet even as he worked, he yearned to belong to a religious order or to be a hermit. He made time to nurture his devout spiritual tendencies and spent long hours in prayer. Before long, he attempted to join the Capuchins but was turned down because of ill health.

Thereafter, Gerard shifted his focus, determined to join the Redemptorists. To prevent Gerard from running away, family members locked him in his room. But the urge was so compelling that Gerard tied his bed linen together to make his escape.

Finally, in 1752, through the intervention of the founder of the Redemptorists, Alphonsus Liguori, Gerard realized his dream and was accepted as a lay brother. During the next three years, he lived a hidden life within the order, performing his religious duties as well as working as a gardener, porter, and tailor. Though his body was weak, he accomplished the work of three. So great was his desire to turn inward to be with God that he suffered self-inflicted pain to keep himself away from the tabernacle. He stood as an exemplary model of every virtue, and even Saint Alphonsus Liguori called him a saint.

Lived—A.D. 1725–1755
Beatified—January 29, 1893
Canonized—December 11, 1904
Feast day—October 16
Patron saint of lay brothers, pregnant women, mothers, unborn children and childbirth

A story is told that a pregnant woman came to Gerard and asked him to pray for her and bless her unborn child that she might not lose the baby. In those days—during the eighteenth century—roughly two-thirds of all pregnancies failed to result in live births. This woman, however, gave birth to a normal, happy baby. Since that time, Gerard has been the one to whom expectant mothers turn to seek blessings and prayers for good births and healthy children.

Roughly three years before Gerard's death, stories began circulating about his profound life of prayer and the gift of grace that he'd been blest with because of his piety, dedication, and discernment. He experienced ecstasies and had the power of prophecy, the stories said. He healed, cast out devils, and converted nonbelievers. And he predicted the day and hour of his death.

Taken ill with tuberculosis, or what some in those times called consumption, Gerard died in the monastery of Caposele, Avellino at the age of 29. Pope Leo XIII beatified him, and Pope Pius X canonized him in 1904. Gerard worked wonders during his lifetime, and some say he remains a wonderworker in death. ✣

WAYS TO HONOR AND INVOKE THE BLESSINGS OF SAINT GERARD MAJELLA

✣ Practice your tailoring skills by making an altar cloth for your own shrine. If you don't sew, you can still make one with fabric, scissors, and trim that can be heat set with an iron and fusing tape.

✣ Work in the garden. Create a beautiful, sacred space in one corner of your garden, backyard, or apartment patio that will be a place to venerate and pray to this saint. Put in plants that give off a sweet scent such as gardenia, certain types of roses, honeysuckle vines, lilacs, and the like. Or plant a "hidden" or night-blooming garden with plants that reveal their beauty only to those who come to perform their prayers or sit in contemplation after the sun goes down.

✣ Serve others. This doesn't have to be some grandiose action. It can be as simple as removing and washing someone's plate or returning a neighbor's garbage can to the yard after a curbside pickup.

✣ Spend some time thinking about this saint's life and what meaning it may hold for your own. Prayerfully petition Saint Gerard Majella for intercession when you feel helpless and hopeless. Never give up, and never forget that the Lord answers our prayers in his own time and way. If you are pregnant, seek this saint's prayers on your behalf for a healthy pregnancy and a safe and normal delivery.

✣ Retreat from distractions of the outer world to go deeply inward in thought, prayer, and meditation. Make a promise to the Lord that you will come to him each day in this way. Remember that Saint Gerard Majella believed that the most important work of the day was making time for God. Spend a few moments of this precious time praising him. Open your heart and invite him in to commune with you. Then, be still and receive.

✣ Do you believe, truly believe, in God's omnipotence and abundance? Talk with him. Ask him for what you need before asking others. Do as Jesus says: "Ask, believing ye shall receive." Perhaps you're in need of emotional sustenance, financial aid, material goods or services, or healing. Consider how all that exists was created by him. Read Genesis and let those words written so long ago lead you deeply inward. Praise God for his mercy, goodness, love, and blessings of abundance and good health.

AFFIRMATIONS

I will bring spiritual time to the beginning and end of each day by spending a few moments in prayer and reflection.

I am integrating new, healthy habits into my life for a more balanced way of living.

I will rise early on [name a day of the week] *to practice mental prayer.*

I seek the company of the Lord before all others.

Prayer to Saint Gerard Majella

O Saint Gerard Majella, whose short life on earth shines as a beacon pointing the way toward God through service, devotion, spiritual practices, and religious duties, pray for us who cannot see our paths as clearly as you did yours.

Pray with us and for us that the Lord may have mercy on the arid desert of our hearts and enable us to find the time, the energy, and the way each and every day to transform our hearts into an oasis of love and devotion in the name of Jesus Christ, our Lord. Pray with us and for us that our love may be like a candle to bring light to the sanctuary of our hearts, our inner temples hidden from view of the world. There may we do our most holy and sacred inner work so that we can be worthy thereafter to go out into the world and minister to one another in his name. Amen.

I SAW A FORM LIKE A LOVELY MAIDEN, HER FACE GLOWING WITH SUCH
RADIANCE THAT I COULD NOT LONG LOOK AT HER. HER GARMENT WAS
WHITER THAN SNOW AND MORE SHINING THAN STARS, AND HER SHOES
WERE MADE OF THE PUREST GOLD.

—HILDEGARD'S DESCRIPTION OF HER VISION
OF THE SACRED FEMININE (FORD-GRABOWSKY, 2002)

HILDEGARD OF BINGEN

How marvelous that the visions and teachings of a twelfth century mystic can have such profound relevance to our lives today. Of her, it can rightfully be said that she gave birth to a kind of sacred femininity that women of modern times have eagerly embraced. But during the Dark Ages, women who, like Hildegard, had visions were considered either mystics or witches (if deemed the latter, their destiny was persecution and death).

While Hildegard believed her revelations and visions came from God, she also knew she would be judged by humans. She felt an urge to write everything down but feared the mockery and criticism that might be levied at her. Somehow, though, she found the strength to trust and honor the sacred voice within.

During her lifetime, Hildegard was a preacher, healer, composer, artist, theologian, and visionary. Today her prodigious legacy of works is a powerful reminder of what we can accomplish once we accept God's sacred gifts and willingly share them with humankind.

Though Hildegard is not a canonized saint, her own biographer Theodoric called her a saint. In addition, many miracles have been claimed in her lifetime and for centuries thereafter as a result of prayers asking for her intercession. In fact, the German town of Eibingen chose her as its patron saint.

Hildegard was the tenth child born to the count and countess of Bermersheim in Böckelheim, Germany. In the Middle Ages, a child might be tithed to the church if, among other reasons, the family was already large. This abandonment, as Hildegard would later reveal in her theological trilogy *Scivias*, was devastating. She was given over to the care of her aunt, the Blessed Jutta von Spanheim, a reclusive spirit and anchoress who lived in a two-room cell that was part of the male Benedictine Saint Disibod's Monastery on the Diessenberg River. Before long, a small monastic community following the rule of Saint Benedict formed and grew. Jutta served as abbess.

During her childhood, Hildegard led a deeply interior life in which she experienced many visions. When she spoke of these experiences to others, their reactions of astonishment made Hildegard reluctant to share such personal spiritual matters. She once asked her nurse if she saw similar things. When the nurse replied no, Hildegard later explained, a great fear befell her.

Lived–A.D. 1098–1179
Not canonized–Named in the Roman Martyrology in the fifteenth century
Feast day–September 17
Patron saint of Eibingen, Germany

At age 15, Hildegard's life as a nun officially began when she was "clothed." After serving for about 17 years, Hildegard, according to some sources, began experiencing ever more powerful visions and revelations. Then, in 1136, Jutta died and Hildegard became prioress. The compelling need to write down her visions grew stronger, but she worried about how they would be perceived. She confessed her concerns to Godfrey, a monk, who took up the issue with his abbot.

The abbot ordered Hildegard to make a written record of some of the visions. He then submitted them to the archbishop of Mainz, who judged them favorably and appointed a monk named Volmar to act as Hildegard's secretary. Those early dictations to Volmar now constitute the beginning of *Scivias*, her book. In it, she reveals 26 visions, illustrating them with sacred feminine imagery—and often employing the pictorial device of women in white robes as allegories for faith, wisdom, peace, truth, justice, and love.

Eventually, the pope, Blessed Eugenius III, upon reviewing a commissioned report on Hildegard's writings, wrote to her and told her to publish whatever the Holy Spirit wished. He warned her, however, against pride, to which Hildegard responded with a long letter warning him against the ambitions of his own household.

Because her monastic community continued to grow, Hildegard began searching for larger accommodations. Between 1147 and 1152, she made her move. Against the wishes of the monks of Saint Disibodenberg (who may have benefited from Hildegard's reputation and the sacred relics of Blessed Jutta), Hildegard relocated her nuns to Rupertsburg, near Bingen, in central Germany. Here she preached reform to lax churches and monasteries. She inspired her 50 nuns to turn the dilapidated church and unfinished buildings into decent housing with water piped throughout.

Sickness was no stranger to Hildegard, but in spite of illness, she continued her prodigious output of creative writing, art, and music. Besides writing plays, poetry, and commentaries on the Gospels, the Rule of Saint Benedict, the lives of saints, and the Athanasian Creed, she also wrote books of medicine and natural history. She produced vivid and radiant artistic renderings of some of her visions. She also wrote music and liturgical hymns, including this antiphon (a hymn to be sung in different parts) to Mary:

*O flowering, noble stem, your flower comes
forth like the dawn.
Rejoice now and be glad, and free us from
evil ways,
Weak as we are—
Stretch out your hand to lift us up.*

—HILDEGARD OF BINGEN
(GLENSTAL ABBEY, 2001)

Hildegard also wrote more than 300 letters to church dignitaries, political leaders, and others. Some letters included prophecies and warnings. Her following of believers grew, while others denounced her as a sorceress.

Hildegard died on September 17, 1179. She was 81. Two attempts, one in the thirteenth and one in the fourteenth century, were made to have her declared a saint. In spite of her theological contributions, she was neither canonized nor made a doctor of the church. ✠

WAYS TO HONOR AND INVOKE THE BLESSINGS OF HILDEGARD OF BINGEN

✠ Make sacred music. Sing spiritual songs as part of your personal daily devotionals. Hildegard did not favor silence imposed upon churches and instead celebrated music as a means to build "a bridge of holiness between this world and the world of all beauty and music."

✠ To align your own spiritual energies and focus, make a black-and-white copy of one or more of the art prints that Hildegard created of her many visions. Using colored pens, chalks, or watercolor, paint her visions and use them as mandalas, or points of departure into contemplation and meditation. Study the symbols, and then read about the piece of art and its spiritual symbolism in books like *Illuminations of Hildegard of Bingen*, by Matthew Fox (Bear & Co., 1985).

✠ God commanded Hildegard to use her sacred gifts. What sacred gifts has God given you? Find out. Form a prayer group with others. Together, support and encourage self-discovery and ways you can share your gifts with humankind.

✠ Watch a video about Hildegard's life. Find videos about her in the National Cathedral bookshop by typing into your computer's search engine the keywords "Hildegard videos". Or purchase the sheet music for hymns she wrote. Locate and listen to tapes or compact discs of her chants. Contact Hildegard Publishing Company, P.O. Box 332, Bryn Mawr, PA 19010.

Prayer to Saint Hildegard

Blessed Saint Hildegard, whose own ecstatic visions of the immeasurable grace and love of our beloved God illuminate our thoughts and inspire our hearts to pursue the divine with unstoppable determination, we seek your prayers on our behalf that our spiritual efforts will rent asunder the veil of darkness so that we, too, may see the sacred light. Help us to seek purity in thought, word, and deed and to offer these holy virtues at the feet of our Lord. Amen.

AD MAJOREM DEI GLORIAM (FOR THE GREATER GLORY OF GOD)

— MOTTO OF IGNATIUS OF LOYOLA AND THE JESUITS

SAINT IGNATIUS OF LOYOLA

If you've ever participated in any kind of spiritual retreat, you already know how powerful that experience can be in bringing about a shift of energy—spiritual, physical, mental, and emotional. Perhaps you've practiced exercises such as visualization, breath work, and mental cleansing to recharge, replenish, and rededicate yourself to a higher good. You may have also spent time in silence, prayer, and performance of service. The point of these activities is to draw you back toward the sacred center of your being…back to God.

Saint Ignatius of Loyola, patron saint of spiritual retreats, clearly understood this aspect of our nature. He wrote a book to help himself, and ultimately it helped more people than he would ever know.

One year before Columbus sailed for America, Iñigo López de Loyola was born into Basque nobility in his family's castle at Azpeita in Guipúzcoa, Spain. The boy, called Ignatius, had seven brothers and three sisters and was the eighth and youngest boy.

His decision to pursue a career in the military was cut short when he was wounded in action. While Ignatius recuperated, he asked for romance novels, something he

loved to read. When there were none to be had, he resigned himself to reading a book about the lives of saints. Now that his days as a military soldier were over, he decided that he, too, could be a soldier for God.

Recovered, he set off on his first pilgrimage, visiting the Shrine of Our Lady of Monserrat near the little town of Manresa. The community had everything he needed—a cave in which to do penance and perform other spiritual practices, a place where he could rest among poor people and beggars, and proximity to some Dominican friars.

Here, in Manresa, where he would stay for the next year, Ignatius began his life as a saint in earnest. He began jotting down ideas and making notes in a journal that would be the beginning of his book *Spiritual Practices*.

In 1523, he decided to make the journey to the Holy Land. He followed a circuitous route that required him to beg all the way and travel by whatever means possible. Eventually, he arrived in Jerusalem with every intention of remaining, but he was warned by a Franciscan to leave or risk being kidnapped for having attempted to convert Moslems.

Ignatius returned to Spain the following year. He decided to pursue further educational studies even while living as a beggar and wearing a habit. He also continued preaching and giving instruction in religious matters (likely based on his *Spiritual*

Lived—A.D. 1491–1556
Canonized—1622
Feast day—July 31
Patron saint of retreats and spiritual exercises

Exercises), and for that he was imprisoned for 42 days by the bishop's vicar general. At issue for Ignatius was whether he belonged to a strange cult of heretics. Eventually, his name was cleared and he was released, but with instructions not to preach for the next three years. He journeyed to a different area of Spain but encountered similar treatment there. By then, however, he had decided to leave Spain and soon departed for France.

In Paris he studied Latin and philosophy, eventually graduating at age 43 with a Master of Arts degree. There he met six individuals: Peter Favre, a newly ordained priest; Francis Xavier, who was a Basque like Ignatius; the scholars Laynez and Salmeron; Simon Rodriguez, a Portuguese national; and Nicholas Bobadilla. On the feast of the Assumption in 1534, these men took holy communion from Peter Favre in the chapel of Saint Denis on Monmartre. Then they pronounced their vows of poverty, chastity, and service as missionaries in Palestine, forming a community that would ultimately become the Society of Jesus.

These first members of the Society of Jesus journeyed to Jerusalem, but Ignatius became ill on the way and returned alone to Spain. Two years later, the group reunited in Venice and from there went to Rome, where those who had not yet been ordained became priests. Pope Paul III approved their religious order in a bull dated September 27, 1540, and Ignatius was elected their first general superior.

The remainder of Ignatius' life was spent in Rome. He oversaw and personally directed the work of his order, including the establishment of universities, colleges, and seminaries. The order grew from the initial seven members to more than 1,000 during Ignatius' lifetime, and it spread throughout Europe and even to Brazil and India.

His book, *Spiritual Exercises*, was published in 1548 with the approval of the pope. The exercises, inspired by a legacy of the writings of predecessors and by his own need, established a means of gaining mastery over oneself. Prayer constituted one rung in his spiritual ladder, which included reading, meditation, prayer, and contemplation (the four stages together are known as Lectio Divina). These steps may have come from Ignatius' reading of *Ladder of Monks* by Guigo II, the Carthusian, a predecessor who set out these four stages. Each step builds upon the preceding ones to reach the final stage of union with God.

Ignatius, who was frequently ill, died unexpectedly on July 31, 1556, too suddenly to even receive the last sacraments. He was 65 years old. More than 200 miracles, including many healings, were attributed to him following his death, and he was canonized in 1622. Centuries later, Pope Pius XI declared him the patron saint of spiritual exercises and retreats. ✢

WAYS TO HONOR AND INVOKE THE BLESSINGS OF SAINT IGNATIUS OF LOYOLA

✢ Purchase or make a beautiful spiritual journal. Vow to write in it every day. Jot down your meditations, inspiring thoughts that come to you in contemplative silence, ideas to further your spiritual development, and notes on how to maximize your activities toward that end. Write messages or poems to your beloved God.

✢ Create a calendar for your spiritual year. Schedule one day each month to review your spiritual progress. Note any special feast days or dates for holy festivities.

✢ Go on a spiritual retreat, if not with your church then by yourself. Take a saint's biography to the beach. Some novitiates and monasteries will allow you go on a retreat at their centers, provided you follow established rules and codes of conduct. Make a date with God.

Prayer to Saint Ignatius of Loyola

Blessed Saint Ignatius of Loyola, who loved Jesus more than life itself and gave your life in service to the Lord, pray for me in this time of distress. Steady my vision and resolve to remain on the path to eternal salvation. Protect me from pitfalls and snares of deception and help me to avoid the great error of sin. Beloved Saint Ignatius of Loyola, your teaching and writing are as a lamp in the darkness our soul passes through. Sanctify our spirits and deepen our devotion to God. Inspire us to follow your example to live a holy life filled with spiritual renewal and ever-new love for Jesus Christ, our Lord. Amen.

THE ANGEL OF THE LORD ENCAMPETH ROUND ABOUT THEM
THAT FEAR HIM, AND DELIVERETH THEM.

— PSALM 34:7

SAINT JOACHIM

Families are challenged in myriad ways. And while problems in the first century did not mirror all of the issues faced by modern families, crises would still have arisen around personal relationships, family interactions, and societal issues. These problems—just as they do today—most certainly would have exacted heavy emotional tolls.

Today, modern Catholics can look upon Saint Joachim and Saint Ann as inspiring examples of two people who personify strength, fortitude, and faith in times of family crises, desperation, fear, and shame.

Not a lot of historical information is available about Joachim, the father of Mary and grandfather of Jesus. Neither he nor Ann, his wife, are mentioned in Scripture. It is probable that he may have been a Nazarene of the Jewish faith. When he was 49, he married Ann, who was 20. Their infertility was seen as a punishment from God and was a source of ridicule and embarrassment in their community.

Some sources suggest that Joachim, if not wealthy, was financially secure. He and Ann were good and pious Jews who divided their income into three parts—the first offered to the temple, the second distributed to the poor, and the third kept for their own needs. Yet their life together produced no child, in spite of their prayers and a promise to consecrate their son or daughter to God. Their community ostracized them for their barrenness, and once the temple even refused Joachim's offering. The reason for this refusal, he was told, was that since he was a sterile man and therefore cursed, he could not stand with men who had fathered sons.

This reproach undoubtedly shamed Joachim deeply. He went into the desert to pray among shepherds and their flocks, avoiding those who mocked him. There, an angel appeared before him, telling him that Ann was carrying a child who was filled with the Holy Spirit. The angel instructed him to name the baby Mary and reminded him of his and Ann's promise to consecrate the child to the Lord. In accordance with the couple's vow to God, when Mary was three, they were to send her to the temple where she would live and learn to serve God.

Lived–First century
Feast day–July 26
Patron saint (with Ann) of parents and grandparents

Joachim was not quite 70 years old when Ann gave birth to Mary. How they must have loved their beautiful daughter for whom they had waited so long and prayed so fervently. To deliver their child to the temple must have been extremely difficult to do. Still, God had blessed them, and for that they would forever be appreciative and grateful. ✦

WAYS TO HONOR AND INVOKE THE BLESSINGS OF SAINTS JOACHIM AND ANN

✦ Be a parent or grandparent to someone by showing love, patience, fortitude, emotional support, spiritual strength, and tenacity of belief in God. If you do not have children or grandchildren, volunteer with social service organizations or church outreach programs that provide companionship and services to seniors and teens.

✦ Create a stunning keepsake book for children or grandchildren, parents or grandparents, in which to keep photos, letters, and other memorabilia. Add a page of your own sweet memories of interacting with any or all of these individuals. Don't forget to make God, Jesus, Mary, Saint Joachim, and Saint Ann part of this book.

✦ Honor God by teaching small ones around you how to love and glorify him. Read from books that introduce them to the saints, teach them prayers, play animated Catholic videos instead of television programs, and make sacred art together.

✝ Set aside a day each week (or half a day) for fasting and prayer. If you are unable to do this for health reasons, "remove" or give up something for those hours. Spend the time in silence and prayer. Read the book of Genesis about how God created the heaven and the earth and everything above and below. From a place of inspiration, create something sacred in honor of his mighty works.

✝ Take a devotional walk around your neighborhood. See God's work in the petals of flowers, in the clouds above you, and in everything you encounter along your path. Thank him for the beauty of the earth, for his artistry and perfection in all things.

AFFIRMATIONS

Evil has no hold on me when the Lord is my guiding light, my polestar, and my beacon in the darkness.

Each week I will spend time in Eucharistic devotion, sending out a call from my soul to God and beckoning him to come to into my heart and make it his permanent dwelling place.

Novena to Saints Joachim and Ann

Saints Joachim and Ann, grandparents of Jesus and parents of Mary, we seek your intercession. We beg you to direct all our actions to the greater glory of God and the salvation of souls. Strengthen us when we are tempted, console us during our trials, help us when we are in need, be with us in life and in death.

O divine Savior, we thank you for having chosen Saints Joachim and Ann to be the parents of our Blessed Mother Mary and so to be your own beloved grandparents. We place ourselves under their patronage this day. We recommend to them our families, our children, and our grandchildren. Keep them from all spiritual and physical harm. Grant that they may ever grow in greater love of God and others.

Saints Joachim and Ann, we have many great needs. We beg you to intercede for us before the throne of your divine Grandson. All of us here have our own special intentions, our own special needs, and we pray that through your intercession our prayers may be granted. Amen.

Recite this novena nine times in a row for nine days in a row.

—CALAMARI AND DIPASQUA, 1999

JOAN WAS A BEING SO UPLIFTED FROM THE ORDINARY RUN OF MANKIND
THAT SHE FINDS NO EQUAL IN A THOUSAND YEARS.

— SIR WINSTON CHURCHILL

SAINT JOAN OF ARC

Joan of Arc was a prisoner of war and was subjected to maltreatment and, many believe, rape. On a mission from God, Joan trusted the King of Heaven, as she called him, and cried out that he alone was to be her judge, a position she did not abdicate even as she was tied to a stake and burned to death.

Born on January 6, 1412 at Domrémy in northeastern France, Joan (or Jehanne, as she was christened) was the child of Jacques d'Arc, a peasant farmer, and his wife Isabelle. The family had three children in all—Joan and two boys. It was from her mother that Joan learned the Our Father, the Hail Mary, and the Apostles Creed.

Joan grew up during the tumultuous Hundred Years War. In 1419, Joan, her family, and another farm family fled to a fortress known as Château de l'Ile on an island in the Meuse, a river running through the valley of farmland and forests that Joan called home. The English army was making a steady, deadly march through France, sacking, looting, and sometimes destroying French villages and towns. The following year, France's rule was divided between

Lived–A.D. 1412–1431
Martyred–Virgin martyr
Beatified–April 11, 1909
Canonized–1920
Feast day–May 30
Special title–Maid of Orleans
Patron saint of France, the military, soldiers, and funeral directors

English King Henry V and France's Duke of Burgundy.

Around this time, Joan had her first numinous vision of brilliant light and voices. To her, the light and the voices seemed "worthy." According to Joan, the voices belonged to God and certain saints, including Catherine of Alexandria and Margaret of Antioch. In vision after vision, Joan said, the voices came to her two or three times a week and instructed her to save France.

While Joan's detractors characterized her as an illiterate girl who'd become hysterical from the trauma of the war being waged all around her, others supported her claims. Then her father had a potent dream in which Joan was the sole woman traveling in the company of men. He interpreted the dream much as anyone in those medieval times would—Joan was to become a prostitute. He quickly made arrangements to marry her off. Joan would have no part of it.

Within two years, she left Domrémy to journey to a neighboring town. There she asked to see Charles de Ponthieu, the young "Dauphin," or claimant to the French throne. It was her plan to accompany the 26-year-old Dauphin to Paris so he could take his rightful place as King Charles VII of France.

By then Joan had begun sharing her prophecies. Naturally, she was considered a laughable fool and a possible heretic—until her prophecies began to come true. Joan's path was quickly cleared for a meeting with the Dauphin, who first had her interrogated by church scholars to ensure she was no heretic. When Joan was granted the titular command of an army, she cut her hair short like that of a court page, donned a suit of armor, and began to lay siege to and capture one town after another. The Dauphin had nothing to lose by allowing Joan to go into battle. If she won, all the better for him, and if she lost, then had not it been her own decision to enter the war?

As it turned out, Joan was victorious. Soon known as the Maid of Orleans, she won battle after battle, eventually clearing the way for the Dauphin to enter the city of Rheims for his coronation on July 17, 1429. The Dauphin took his rightful place on the throne and was crowned King Charles VII. When Joan captured Saint-Pierre-le-Moutier, Charles bestowed noble status upon Joan and her family.

Yet victory in battle, as Joan herself knew, would not be her final act. Predicting that she would lose the battle of Compiègne in May 1430, Joan fought nonetheless. As foretold, she was captured by the Burgundians and handed over to the English.

King Charles VII never bothered to intervene on Joan's behalf, even when she was tried by pro-English clergy and convicted in 1431 of heresy. Joan was sentenced to burn at the stake. More than one source has suggested that during her questioning and imprisonment, she was starved, deprived of sleep, and raped.

Joan was a mere 19 years old when she was led to the marketplace in Rouen to be burned to death. On the way, she implored God to save her. During the burning, she focused her attention on a cross and uttered the name of Jesus. The Seine became the final resting place for her ashes.

It took 25 years for Joan's family to get the charges of heresy reversed. Only after a lengthy re-trial known as the Rehabilitation Trial and another 500 years could Joan at last be canonized. In England's Winchester Cathedral, her statue stands opposite the tomb of Cardinal Beaufort, who participated in her condemnation. ✛

…But God hath chosen the foolish things of the world to confound the wise; and God hath chosen the weak things of the world to confound the things which are mighty.

—I CORINTHIANS 1:27

WAYS TO HONOR AND INVOKE THE BLESSINGS OF SAINT JOAN OF ARC

✛ Offer to do some art with a woman who needs support. Encourage her to use art as a means to release emotions or to tap into a higher and more sacred energy. For example, design and decorate a floor cloth as a sacred rug on which to sit or kneel for prayers.

✛ Before going to bed, light a candle. Breathe out deeply, letting go of all the stress and worries you've acquired through-out the day. Ask forgiveness for your "tres-passes" against others. Then ask forgiveness for those who have "trespassed against you." Once this releasing is done, try to feel the sacredness of this one moment. Express gratitude to God for your blessings and then pray for those blessings to be show-ered on all others.

✛ Imagine what Joan of Arc went through when she was betrayed, tried, and burned at the stake. If you, like Joan, caught sight of a cross nearby, would you, in your pain and agony, stay focused on its meaning? How might this exercise have relevance in the trials of your own life?

AFFIRMATIONS

As I go about my work at home and in the world, may my words be sweet, my smile infectious, and my diligence contagious.

I am a soldier of God in the fight for moral righteousness.

Lord, I am thy torchbearer. Use me to bring light wherever there is darkness in my community and country.

✛✛✛✛✛✛✛✛✛✛✛✛✛✛✛✛✛✛✛✛✛✛

Rape Survivor's Prayer to Saint Joan of Arc

Maid of Orleans, Saint Joan of Arc, your prayers are needed for this poor soul who has been accosted. Pray that she finds peace and courage to get through this terrible ordeal. Ask the Lord to give her the bravery that you found in battle. May God provide her with support from family and friends and instill upon her a warmth and gentleness that she may have lost. In his powerful name we pray. Amen.

—PHILIP LIEF GROUP, INC., 2003

✛✛✛✛✛✛✛✛✛✛✛✛✛✛✛✛✛✛✛✛✛✛

ARE NOT FIVE SPARROWS SOLD FOR TWO FARTHINGS, AND NOT ONE
OF THEM IS FORGOTTEN BEFORE GOD? BUT EVEN THE VERY HAIRS
OF YOUR HEAD ARE ALL NUMBERED. FEAR NOT THEREFORE: YE ARE OF
MORE VALUE THAN MANY SPARROWS.

— LUKE 12:6–7

SAINT JOHN OF GOD

How do we walk that fine line between honoring and cherishing the bodies, minds, and hearts of others and also preserving our own in the same way? We have a duty to do both. To dishonor our bodies is to dishonor the interior temple in which we worship God.

Saint John of God went insane for the love of God and was committed to an asylum. Upon his release from the institution, he found a way to give outward expression to his deep spiritual yearnings and to help the sick and indigent along the way.

John was born at Monte Mor il Nuovo in Portugal in 1495. He worked for the Count of Oroprusa as a youth. Then, at age 27, he joined the mercenaries serving the Count and fought for Spain against the French and the Turks. He abandoned his religion while in military service, but when the troop disbanded and he went to Andalusia to work as a shepherd, he began to feel remorse for his lapse. When he turned 40 years of age, John began to consider what, in the service of God, he could do with the rest of his life. He decided to help Christian slaves in Africa and soon headed for Gibraltar.

In Gibraltar, John worked the streets, pedaling sacred art and texts. Early success propelled him into opening his own shop in Granada. On Saint Sebastian's feast day, John attended a lecture by a famous preacher named John of Àvila. The sermon so touched John, the seller of art and books, that he made a scene, beating his chest and crying out loudly in the church. He tore at his hair, ran out into the streets, and made his way to his shop, where he gave everything away. Then he wandered the streets aimlessly until someone took pity and escorted him into the presence of John of Àvila.

The meeting went well enough, and John calmed as the holy man, John of Àvila, talked quietly, offering help and suggesting that John give himself over to serving the poor and caring for the sick. Before long, however, John was again behaving like a mad man, and authorities took him to an asylum for the insane. There he was treated according to the brutal methods thought at the time to be effective in restoring sanity.

John of Àvila visited the patient and again gave advice, this time instructing John to find constructive activity that would benefit his own spiritual progress as well as help others. John of God became a helper in the hospital where he was confined, working there until Saint Ursula's day in 1539.

Lived–A.D. 1495–1550
Canonized–1690
Feast day–March 8
Patron saint of heart patients, hospitals, booksellers, and printers

After John left the hospital, he scavenged for firewood and sold it, using the money he made to feed the poor. In time, he contracted for a house where he allowed sick and poor people to stay. This venture proved as successful as John's book-selling efforts. The home for the poor and house for the sick was to become the foundation of the order of Brothers of Saint John of God.

John worked diligently over the next decade, attending to the physical as well as spiritual needs of his patients. He even saved a man from a flood, along with the wood and items John had gathered and stored for the poor. After this heroic effort, however, he fell ill. For some time, he concealed his illness, but in time he died, kneeling before the altar in the chapel of his hospital. He was 55 years old. The archbishop arranged the burial, and the townspeople of Granada walked in the funeral procession to honor John of God.

Never during his life did John plan to develop a religious order, but a community of his followers drew up rules some six years after his death, naming John of God their founder. Some 14 or 15 years later, they at last took their formal religious vows. ✝

WAYS TO HONOR AND INVOKE THE BLESSINGS OF SAINT JOHN OF GOD

✝ Volunteer at a hospital or clinic for the sick or indigent. Something as simple as delivering a magazine, helping someone eat a meal, or serving as a watchful guardian at the bedside of an ill person make all the difference to a patient and to members of the family.

✝ Help out at an Alzheimer center. Talk with the center's activities director to see if you can assist during field trips or with special planned activities.

✝ Offer to give a break to a caretaker. The responsibility of caring for someone who is dying, suffering dementia, or growing infirm with age makes great demands on care givers. These people need an hour here and there to conduct the business of their own lives or to sit in a garden, take a walk, or just think or pray.

✝ Say prayers to honor Saint John of God. Emulate his life by helping in small ways to care for the sick and the poor.

✝ Give any unwanted sacred books and art to a worthy charitable cause.

✣ Vow to be truthful in every way for one day. Before you speak, think twice about what you will say. As you go through the tasks of your day and interact with others, consider how often you might "fudge" the truth, speak a half-truth, or embellish the truth, even when your motive is well intentioned. At the end of this day, spend a little quiet time reviewing what you have learned about yourself by going through this process.

✣ Imagine the Lord as your beloved. When two lovers are apart, all they want to do is think about being together again. Consider how you might develop that kind of deep devotion and attachment to the Lord. Think, also, about how Saint John of God so loved the Lord that he lost his sanity. In many ways, being in love makes you crazy. You may feel drunk with desire. You may even wish you could merge yourself with the soul of your lover. Imagine feeling that way toward the Lord. Write a love letter to God.

AFFIRMATIONS

I am setting aside my ego to allow the Lord to use the instruments of my body and my mind for the benefit of those who are sick, poor, abused, or tortured.

I will be a magnifier for the abundance in my life, giving what I can each day to others, even if it is just my smile.

I will carry out my role in life according to God's plan, not wasting the moments given to me in idle pursuits, but using them to deepen my spiritual focus and efforts.

✣✣✣✣✣✣✣✣✣✣✣✣✣✣✣✣✣✣✣✣✣✣✣

Prayer to Saint John of God

Most holy Saint John of God, faithful servant and friend of the poor and the infirm, your burning love for God and feelings of charity for all his less fortunate children made you worthy of his grace and miraculous powers. I implore you to intercede for me to Lord Jesus that I may learn to better cherish this body through which I am able to do his work by caring for others. May I be worthy of his grace and love, and may I be able to awaken in the hearts of others an acceptance of the teachings of our Lord. Grant this petition and I promise to strive always to do God's will and hold the gratitude I feel for you forever in my heart. Amen.

✣✣✣✣✣✣✣✣✣✣✣✣✣✣✣✣✣✣✣✣✣✣✣

GOD PASSES THROUGH THE THICKET OF THE WORLD,
AND WHEREVER HIS GLANCE FALLS, HE TURNS ALL THINGS TO BEAUTY.

— SAINT JOHN OF THE CROSS

SAINT JOHN OF THE CROSS

Our modern society discounts age, timelessness, wisdom, and beauty. What if we used a different yardstick—one that measures a person's life against levels achieved in spiritual prowess, virtuous living, and evolution of the soul? In a scenario such as that, where a contemplative life is highly valued, Saint John of the Cross stands as a giant.

John was born Juan de Yepes on June 24, 1542 at Fontiveros, Old Castile. His parents were noble but quite poor because his father had been disinherited for marrying below his rank. Gonzalo de Yepes, John's father, and his mother, Catherine Alvarez, eked out a living as silk weavers. When his father died, leaving John to be raised by his mother, the two of them moved to Medina del Campo.

John attended poor school there and was soon apprenticed to an artisan, a carpenter, and a printer. He showed little aptitude for any of these trades, even though he was a diligent and attentive student. So, with the help of a local hospital administrator, a new plan was devised: John would be his servant and would work at the hospital, caring for the sick and infirm while simultaneously studying at a school established by the Jesuits. The hospital administrator hoped that John would become a priest and return to the hospital as its chaplain.

In 1563, John joined the Carmelites after receiving guidance during prayer that suggested he serve God by joining an order that he could return to its ancient perfection. Now calling himself John of Saint Matthias, he asked for and received permission to leave the group and practice his faith in the original Carmelite traditions, without all the changes put in place by others and granted by various popes.

After traveling to Salamanca to study theology, John became an ordained priest in 1567. It was then he began to embrace the idea of joining the Carthusian Order, but he was persuaded by Teresa of Àvila to join the Discalced Reform instead. Teresa had been sent to Medina to establish a convent for nuns and was authorized to also establish two houses for friars to carry out the primitive rule. John decided to give this a try.

He took two companions with him to the small house that had been offered in Valladolid. Around this time, he began calling himself Saint John of the Cross. He and his companions began practicing their reformed ways in 1568. As a Discalced Carmelite, John worked at various posts until he was beckoned to Àvila to become the confessor to the nuns at the motherhouse of Teresa's reformed order.

Lived–A.D. 1542–1591
Beatified–1675
Canonized–1726
Feast day–December 14 (formerly November 24)
Special title–Doctor of Mystical Theology
Patron saint of mystics and poets

In 1577, John was imprisoned by the Calced (as opposed to the Discalced) Carmelites following a general meeting of Calced friars who opposed reform and refused to give their various houses' independence. The abysmal conditions of his confinement in a narrow, dark, unventilated cell in Toledo, a cell that was freezing in the cold months and stiflingly hot in the summer, only spurred him to turn inward. Starved and flogged by those who were trying to convince him to leave the Discalceds, John remained steadfast in his beliefs. During those nine months, after a jailer took pity on him and brought writing supplies and a candle, John wrote some of his most lyrical and mystical poetry.

In August 1578, John made his escape by loosening the lock on his cell door and using two rugs twisted into a rope. Barefoot and covered with all manner of vermin, he struggled to make his way to the nunnery. There the women took him in, nursed his wounds, and hid him from authorities.

Once recovered, John was sent to be the prior and confessor to the Discalced nuns at the house of El Calvario, near Baeza. He established several friaries and, from 1579 to 1582, served as rector of the Carmelite college at Baeza. From 1588 on, he wrote his most notable works: *The Ascent of Mount Carmel, The Spiritual Canticle, The Living Flame of Love, and The Dark Night of the Soul.*

Teresa, until her death in 1582, was one of his greatest supporters. In her absence, John faced fractious opposition from the Discalceds and the Carmelites of the Ancient Observance. No longer elected to any offices, John was sent to a remote friary in southern Spain to be forgotten. He fell ill, and simultaneously, it seems, news came that he was to be expelled from the order. John was subsequently sent to yet another friary at Ubeda, where he was treated badly by the prior. John died there on December 15, 1591.

In 1926, 335 years after his death, John was declared a Doctor of the Church. During his life, he had come to believe that practicing asceticism purified the soul, preparing it for the deep mystical union with God. He is remembered as a man of small physical stature whom God magnified in greatness. ✝

✠ Search out and read the poems of Saint John of the Cross; then write your own poem to honor some aspect of God. Transcribe it onto beautiful, handmade paper or make it into a piece of needlepoint and frame it.

✠ Close your eyes and listen to the composer Samuel Barber's beautiful "Adagio for Strings". Imagine, as the music begins its melodic ascent, that it is carrying your soul to its source.

✠ Walk barefoot for a day and be aware of how your feet connect with surfaces bearing your weight—the floor, earth, or grass. Use the idea of God supporting you and infusing you with subtle energy through his creations as a departure point to begin writing in a journal or to start a meditation.

✠ Spend some time contemplating the mystical union of your soul with the Lord. Begin with a visualization of being lovingly held in the sacred heart. Imagine yourself bathed in warm light and feeling the bliss of divine love.

Prayer to Saint John of the Cross

O Saint John of the Cross, who lived in a way to purify the earthly dross from your body and soul to make it ready for union with God, we seek your loving support in our own efforts toward that goal. Though learned, your way of knowing God's truth was by direct experience rather than through the influence of others. Pray for us that we gain insight into any offensive aspects of ourselves. Intercede for us as we petition him to bless us with his loving grace. Through our ongoing efforts, may we one day be found pure enough to enter into that mystical union that we deeply desire. Amen.

AND THOU SHALT HAVE JOY AND GLADNESS, AND MANY WILL REJOICE
AT HIS BIRTH. FOR HE SHALL BE GREAT IN THE SIGHT OF THE
LORD, AND SHALL DRINK NEITHER WINE NOR STRONG DRINK:
AND HE SHALL BE FILLED WITH THE HOLY GHOST.

— LUKE 1:14–16

SAINT JOHN THE BAPTIST

Humility seems to have fallen out of fashion. It was once a highly prized virtue--but seems to have been replaced with competitive one-upmanship and shameless self-promotion. What happened to humility? One fine example from Biblical history of someone who exemplified perfect humility was Saint John the Baptist.

John was born during the reign of Herod in the first century and was the son of Zechariah, a priest with the priestly division of Abijah, and Elizabeth, who was one of the daughters of Aaron and a cousin to the Virgin Mary. It was to Elizabeth's house in the city of Judah in the hill country that Mary first went after she learned she was pregnant with Jesus. And it was to Elizabeth that Mary first spoke the words of what is known as the Canticle of Mary, praising God.

John's parents were good Jews who fault-lessly observed all the commandments, ordinances, and rituals of Mosaic Law, yet they remained a barren couple despite trying most of their married life to conceive. People of that time would have called their barrenness a curse and put the blame on the couple for displeasing God. In the case of John's parents, however, just the opposite was true. God was about to bless them in a glorious way.

One day Zechariah was alone in the temple lighting the incense, one of his priestly duties, when the angel Gabriel appeared to him with news of God's great blessing to come. He told Zechariah not to fear but to rejoice, because God had heard his many prayers. The angel promised the couple would soon have a son, and Zechariah, who had difficulty believing the angel, was struck dumb. As he went out from the temple, people addressed him, perhaps to ask what had taken so long, but he said nothing, not then nor in the months that followed.

John (from the Hebrew Jehohanan, meaning "Jahweh has mercy") was born about six months before Jesus. "And it came to pass, that on the eighth day they came to circumcise the child, and they called him Zechariah, after the name of his father. And his mother answered and said, Not so; but he shall be called John." (Luke 1: 59–60)

There were those who protested that the name was not a fitting one, for there was no one in Elizabeth's or Zechariah's family with that name. So Zechariah was asked to make the final decision. He wrote on a piece of paper, "His name is John," (Luke 1:63) and suddenly Zechariah could again speak. His first words were to praise God.

Lived–First century
Feast day–June 24
Second feast day–August 29 (for his death by beheading)
Patron saint of monks, the city of Florence, Jordan, candle makers, road workers, wool workers, and leatherworkers

The Gospel of Luke says that John "grew, and waxed strong in spirit, and was in the deserts till the day of his shewing unto Israel." (Luke 1:80) Whether John stayed in the desert to escape death at the hands of Herod or to simply grow closer to God in spirit and consciousness isn't known. But it is known that he lived like an anchorite or hermit and, when he turned 30, entered public ministry.

John the Baptist was a fierce-looking ascetic in his camel-hair shirt girded at the waist with leather. His oratory was as fiery as an Old Testament prophet, and he drew large crowds with his preaching. One day, among those who came to hear him was his cousin Jesus. As John had done for so many others, he baptized Jesus but reportedly said that it was he, John, who needed baptism from his cousin. John lived up to his reputation for humility when he told his own disciples to follow Jesus—that Jesus must now increase while he, John, must decrease.

John was also vocal about people who gave in to base instincts and immoral practices. He denounced the sexual union of Herod Antipas with Herodias, his niece and brother's wife. This incurred the wrath of Herodias. When Herod promised Salomé, daughter of Herodias, anything she desired in exchange for her dancing, Salomé, who'd been coached by her mother, asked for the head of John the Baptist on a platter. Herod was delighted to have an excuse to be rid of a preacher so popular

with the masses and a threat to Herod's power. He happily indulged Salomé's request.

Upon learning of the death of his cousin, Jesus spoke about John in loving words, praising him and saying that while no man on Earth was greater than John, in the kingdom of heaven the least among men was greater than John in the sight of God.

John was buried in Samaria. His reputation as a monk has always been held in high esteem. In the Middle Ages, there were more than 496 churches dedicated to him. He knew his destiny was to prepare the way for the coming of Christ. When the time came for John to give all glory to Jesus, he did it without hesitation. ✣

WAYS TO HONOR AND INVOKE THE BLESSINGS OF SAINT JOHN THE BAPTIST

✣ Share the word of God with others.

✣ Find ways each day to let go of pride and replace it with humility. That is not to say you can't feel good about your accomplishments. Just be humble.

✣ Practice not being attached to the outcome of the work you do. Mentally give over all the accolades and the fruit of all labor to God, the unseen doer working through you.

✣ On Saint John's feast day, serve snails in spicy tomato sauce, as they do in Rome, or fry fish as they do in Formia (theirs is fish from the Adriatic).

The Canticle of Zechariah (Luke 1:68–79)

Blessed be the Lord God of Israel; for he hath visited and redeemed his people,

And hath raised up a horn of salvation for us in the house of his servant David;

As he spake by the mouth of his holy prophets, which have been since the world began:

That we should be saved from our enemies and the hand of all that hate us;

To perform the mercy promised to our fathers, and to remember the holy covenant;

The oath which he swore to our father Abraham,

That he would grant unto us, that we, being delivered out of the hand of our enemies, might serve him without fear,

In holiness and righteousness before him, all the days of our life.

And thou, child, shalt be called the prophet of the Highest, for thou shalt go before the face of the Lord to prepare his ways;

To give knowledge of salvation unto his people by the remission of their sins,

Through the tender mercy of our God; whereby the dayspring from on high hath visited us,

To give light to them that sit in darkness and in the shadow of death, to guide our feet into the way of peace.

Prayer to Saint John the Baptist

Blessed Saint John, who fulfilled Scripture and baptized our Savior, pray for us who wish to share the word of God with those souls who have not yet come to him. May our petitions be blessed by your loving heart and delivered to our Lord Jesus that we may speak with the power of the passion and devotion you felt for God while on earth. May those who hear our voice be turned from darkness toward the light of Christ. Amen.

BUT WHILE HE THOUGHT ON THESE THINGS, BEHOLD, THE ANGEL OF
THE LORD APPEARED UNTO HIM IN A DREAM, SAYING, JOSEPH, THOU SON
OF DAVID, FEAR NOT TO TAKE UNTO THEE MARY THY WIFE: FOR THAT
WHICH IS CONCEIVED IN HER IS OF THE HOLY GHOST.

— MATTHEW 1:20

SAINT JOSEPH

When Joseph learned that Mary, the young woman betrothed to him, was pregnant, he decided not to publicly denounce her but rather to quietly divorce her. This was an act of compassion, for he knew only too well that any infidelity of a betrothed woman would be punished with death by stoning according to Mosaic Law.

Joseph didn't rush to judge Mary but instead sought to protect her from shame. How easy it would have been for him to feel betrayed, angry, and hurt, perhaps even to consider ways to get even. Sound familiar? How often we jump to conclusions, choosing to believe the worst about someone, even a loved one. But Joseph's example shows how we can stay on the moral high ground through compassion and reason.

The Gospel of Saint Luke says Joseph was born in Bethlehem but lived in Nazareth with Mary. But the Gospel of Saint Matthew suggests that Joseph and Mary lived in Bethlehem and then moved to Nazareth after they had fled into Egypt to protect Jesus from Herod.

Joseph, a carpenter of humble means even though he was descended from King David, is depicted in most texts as a loving father and faithful husband. His job was nothing less than to protect the holy family and oversee the upbringing of Jesus. At the circumcision ceremony in the temple, when Jesus was presented to the Lord, Joseph offered the sacrifice of a pair of turtledoves. This was in accordance with the law of the Lord, and Joseph abided by those laws. He also taught young Jesus how to use the tools and techniques of his trade, thus providing Jesus with an honorable trade. But, of course, God had other plans for the work Jesus would do.

When Jesus was 12, Joseph and Mary took him along as they journeyed to Jerusalem for the feast of Passover. When it was over, the couple began the journey home, thinking that Jesus was in the caravan with them. When they couldn't find him, they quickly returned to Jerusalem, frantically searching for their lost child at the homes of relatives and friends. Finally, after three days, the anxious couple located him in the temple, conversing with the learned men and rabbis.

Lived–First century
Feast day–Third Wednesday after Easter, or March 19, for the Solemnity of Joseph
Second feast day–May 1, for Joseph the Worker
Patron saint of carpenters, manual laborers, a holy death, fathers of families, Korea, Vietnam, China, Austria, Russia, Belgium, procurators, and bursars (treasurers)

And when they saw him, they were amazed: and his mother said unto him, Son, why hast thou thus dealt with us? Behold, thy father and I have sought thee sorrowing.

— LUKE 2:48

Jesus, of course, replied that he had simply been about his "Father's business." The Bible says that both parents found him in the temple but describes only Mary's reaction. Perhaps Joseph felt that it was not his place to speak out. Or perhaps he was contemplating the meaning and spiritual significance of the situation rather than reacting to it. That would have been Joseph's way.

After recounting that journey to Jerusalem, the New Testament does not mention Joseph again. Some Biblical scholars suggest that he may have died before Jesus began to teach and openly minister to others.

Saints, including Saint Teresa of Àvila, Saint Francis de Sales, and Saint Ignatius of Loyola, have for centuries venerated Saint Joseph. In 1870, during the First Vatican Council, Pope Pius IX proclaimed Saint Joseph patron saint of the universal church. In art, Joseph is often depicted alongside Mary and Jesus, and his name has always been a popular choice for baptisms and confirmations. ✛

WAYS TO HONOR AND INVOKE THE BLESSINGS OF SAINT JOSEPH

✛ Ask God to bless your heart as he did Joseph's with the grace of supernatural love so that you can love as Joseph did. Make this prayer part of your daily devotions and put that love into practice by giving it to those who need it most in your family, in your church, and in your community.

✛ Write an affirmation in which you promise God that you will not be judgmental or critical of others. Tape the affirmation to your bathroom mirror and say it often. Replace the negative habit of criticism with a positive habit of expressing love and understanding. Remember the counsel of Proverbs 2:11, "Discretion shall preserve thee, understanding shall keep thee...."

✛ Buy or make a keepsake box made of wood. Sketch or transfer a lovely pattern on the lid and then carve the pattern with woodcarving tools. Think of how carefully Joseph may have guided the small hands of Jesus in his workshop as he taught the boy about carpentry, life skills, and good habits. As you succeed in changing your own bad habits into good ones through your affirmations, remove the affirmations from your mirror and store them in this box, along with your messages to Saint Joseph asking for his intercessory prayers to the Lord.

✛ Avoid automatic reactions. Allow time to reflect on and reason out each situation before reacting to it, as Saint Joseph surely would have done.

✛ Strive to build strong spiritual families. When someone feels like a failure, kindle new strength within that person. Share the most direct route to God that you have found. Be a witness for the Lord God in all your relationships, but especially within your own family. God created man and woman, and the two of them become "one body," the book of Genesis tells us.

Whether or not you have a partner in life, use this idea of two becoming one as a point of departure into contemplation of how to turn divisiveness into oneness and unity.

✛ Be present for a child. You may find this more challenging with teenagers whose developmental task is to break away and become separate individuals. Life in our modern world can be tough on kids. Temptations scream out to them daily. Be there for them. Show them how to be fathers, mothers, leaders, supporters, and friends.

Novena to Saint Joseph

Saint Joseph, you are the faithful protector and intercessor of all who love and venerate you. I have special confidence in you. You are powerful with God and will never abandon your faithful servants.

I humbly invoke you and commend myself, with all who are dear to me, to your intercession. By the love you have for Jesus and Mary, do not abandon me during life, and assist me at the hour of my death.

Glorious Saint Joseph, spouse of the immaculate Virgin, foster-father of Jesus Christ, obtain for me a pure, humble, and charitable mind and perfect resignation to the Divine Will. Be my guide, my father, and my model through life that I may merit to die as you did in the loving arms of Jesus and Mary.

Loving Saint Joseph, faithful follower of Jesus Christ, I raise my heart to you to implore your powerful intercession in obtaining from the heart of Jesus all the graces necessary for my spiritual and temporal welfare, particularly the grace of a happy death, and the special grace I now implore: (mention your request).

Guardian of the Word Incarnate, I am confident that your prayers on my behalf will be graciously heard before the throne of God. Amen.

Recite this novena nine times in a row for nine days in a row.

— LOVASIK, 2000

JUDAS SAITH UNTO HIM, NOT ISCARIOT, LORD, HOW IS IT THAT THOU WILT MANIFEST THYSELF UNTO US, AND NOT UNTO THE WORLD? JESUS ANSWERED AND SAID UNTO HIM, IF A MAN LOVE ME, HE WILL KEEP MY WORDS: AND MY FATHER WILL LOVE HIM, AND WE WILL COME UNTO HIM AND MAKE OUR ABODE WITH HIM.

— JOHN 14:22–23

SAINT JUDE

Are you in a seemingly hopeless situation with no obvious way out? Do you know someone who is? Pray a novena to Saint Jude, the patron saint of impossible and desperate cases. Many people have petitioned him with good results. Every day, small ads of thanks appear in newspapers to testify to the intercessory powers of this saint.

One of the 12 apostles of Jesus, Jude Thaddaeus (or Judas, not to be confused with Judas Iscariot, who betrayed the Lord) is believed by some to have been the brother of James the Less, although this is disputed by other scholars, and a cousin of Jesus. He was with Jesus from earliest childhood and remained faithful to him as an adult.

His name is often used with the surname name of Thaddaeus, and he is frequently mentioned with Saint Simon (who in art is often depicted holding a fish). Jude is sometimes pictured with a ship because he traveled over water to lands where he did missionary work.

Most sources suggest that because Jude's name was often confused with the other Judas, no one ever invoked Saint Jude in any petition, and he became the saint of the impossible. Essentially forgotten in the Middle Ages, there has been a huge resurgence of interest in this saint because, when he answers the prayers of those in dire circumstances, those individuals must publish a small ad in a newspaper to thank him for his intercession. Most papers contain many of these small thank-you notices to Saint Jude.

There is little information to be found about him in any of the gospels. In sacred art and on religious candle images, he is depicted with the Holy Spirit's flame ever burning over his head and with a large stick or club in his hand, for a club was the weapon used to kill him.

Saint Jude was martyred with Saint Simon in Persia while preaching the gospel. His relics were moved to Saint Peter's in Rome around the seventh or eighth century. Others of his relics went to Reims and Toulouse. ✟

Lived–First century
Martyred–First century
Feast day–June 19
Patron saint of hopeless causes

And when they were come in, they went up into an upper room, where abode both Peter, and James, and John, and Andrew, Philip, and Thomas, Bartholomew, and Matthew, James the son of Alpheus, and Simon Zelotes, and Judas, the brother of James. These all continued with one accord in prayer and supplication, with the women, and Mary the mother of Jesus, and with his brethren.

— ACTS 1:13–14

WAYS TO HONOR AND INVOKE THE BLESSINGS OF SAINT JUDE

✙ Perform a prayerful and loving act of kindness for someone (especially a child) suffering from a debilitating disease.

✙ Wear a Saint Jude miraculous medal.

✙ Purchase or make your own religious candle in honor of Saint Jude. Light it and say a novena to Saint Jude nine times in a row for nine days in row.

✙ Volunteer with a hospice and give comfort to the terminally ill and to their loved ones.

✙ Work toward healing from the inside out. Lie on a flat surface. Close your eyes. Breathe in to the count of three and exhale to the count of six. Let go of all tension completely. Relax your entire body. Then see your disease, pain, or physical problem as dark spots in your body of light. Put your attention on the point of pain. Breathe in. See these dark spots coalesce into a giant black blob. Breathe out and with the outgoing breath see the dark blob moving outward, away from you into space. Breathe naturally now and watch the black blob grow smaller and smaller until it is a spot on the horizon, leaving the atmosphere, the solar system. With each breath in, imagine your body refilling with life-giving particles of light. Imagine these particles are healthy new cells. Let the light warm and energize you. Feel healthy, whole, and healed. Seal this moment in your thoughts and return to it again and again throughout the day.

✣ When you are feeling far removed from your spiritual center, water the arid desert of your heart by reading the psalms, which have been called a "school of prayer." Allow one or more of these "prayers" to lead you inward. Voice your own hopes, dreams, and deepest feelings. Choose a psalm for healing or one for wisdom. Memorize a meaningful verse.

AFFIRMATIONS

I yoke the power of thought to my force of will to achieve my goals.

I place my faith in the healing power of the Lord, and I will do my part to properly care for my body and mind and uphold the laws of nature. In this way, I am becoming healthier each day.

Given the choice between seeking God or God's gifts, I will always choose seeking God.

Prayer for Healing

Blessed Saint Jude, I am in great distress. I feel as if my life is ebbing away. I seek healing from our Lord God, the source of all healing. I am in great peril. In my heart I know that a single loving thought from the Lord or a mere glance from his loving eyes can instantly redeem and restore me. I pray for your intercession on my account and ask you to pray with me and for me to the Lord that he will feel compassion toward me and heal my affliction. Amen.

Prayer to Saint Jude

O Saint Jude, friend and holy apostle who devoted your life to serving Jesus and spreading his teachings, pray for me and with me to our Lord that a swift resolution might be found for my great need. I feel so desperately alone and afraid. Saint Jude, you are my last resort. Please help me (mention your request). Hear and carry my prayer for assistance that our loving God might have mercy upon me. I will honor you, Saint Jude, and forever be grateful for your favor. Amen.

AND ANANIAS WENT HIS WAY, AND ENTERED INTO THE HOUSE:
AND PUTTING HIS HANDS ON HIM, SAID, BROTHER SAUL, THE LORD,
EVEN JESUS, THAT APPEARED UNTO THEE IN THE WAY AS THOU CAMEST,
HATH SENT ME, THAT THOU MIGHTEST RECEIVE THY SIGHT, AND BE
FILLED WITH THE HOLY GHOST.

— ACTS 9:17–18

SAINT LUCY

Many times in the gospels we find sight (and also light) used as a metaphor for spiritual breakthrough, while blindness (or darkness) becomes a metaphor for spiritual ignorance. Therefore, when we read the stories of the gospels, it's always good to see if deeper meaning can be fathomed from interpreting them on two levels: outward and inward. Sight and light call to mind one of Christianity's most adored saints—Saint Lucy, whose main attributes are lucidity and light. Even her name derives from the Latin word for light, lux.

References to Saint Lucy can be found in the some of the oldest Roman religious records. She was born into a wealthy Sicilian family in Syracuse, Sicily in the year A.D. 285. As was the norm for that era, her family arranged for her to be married.

Inspired by the martyred Saint Agatha, Lucy instead promised her body and mind to Christ. Much to the consternation of her betrothed, she desired that items of her dowry be given to the poor and needy. Lucy pledged to live a chaste life devoted to prayer.

In those days of Diocletian persecutions, someone had only to report to the authorities that a person was a Christian, and punishment in the form of torture and death would be duly meted out. Christian women were routinely tortured by being sent to serve time in a brothel.

Lucy's spurned suitor reported her, and when she was called before the Roman consul Paschasius to answer the charges that she refused to sacrifice to the Roman idols, she spoke of sacrifice as more important for the poor than for idols. This angered the official, and he ordered her sent to a brothel.

When the soldiers came to escort her to the brothel, they found that she had become immobile, and they could not move her. Reinforcements were sent, along with oxen, but still Lucy could not be budged. Paschasius had his men build a funeral pyre around her and torch it. Still, Lucy was immovable. She said she wanted nonbelievers to have the opportunity to curse and insult her and believers to have their fears of suffering and death assuaged.

Lived–A.D. 285–304
Martyred–Virgin martyr
Feast day–December 13
Patron saint of the blind and those with eye problems, hemorrhages, and throat ailments and also of authors

Enraged, Paschasius ordered one of his men to thrust his sword across Lucy's neck, cutting her throat. Reputedly, before she died, her eyes were cut out but were miraculously restored. As news of Lucy's martyrdom spread, her cult swelled in numbers, as did stories of miraculous healing. Churches dedicated to her sprung up all over Italy and as far away as England (albeit several centuries later).

People of Sweden celebrate her feast on the shortest day of the year and call it their festival of light. In art, Lucy is often depicted holding her eyes on a tray. ✟

WAYS TO HONOR AND INVOKE THE BLESSINGS OF SAINT LUCY

✟ Become immovable like Saint Lucy after committing yourself to a spiritual goal, such as saying the rosary every morning. Don't let anything move you from that commitment.

✟ Form a Bible study group to bring light and greater understanding to the words you read in Scripture and those you say in prayer. Try to fathom deeper meaning. In the Middle Ages, clerics reportedly spent untold hours just trying to decipher the full meaning from such words as Ave, which begins the church's greatest devotional prayer: Ave, Maria, gratia plena; Dominus tecum (Hail, Mary, full of grace; the Lord is with thee).

✟ Offer to do readings from books for a charitable organization that serves the needs of the blind.

✟ Perform a prayerful and loving act of kindness for someone suffering from macular degeneration or any other form of eye disease. Say a prayer to Saint Lucy for that person.

✟ Make the Italian sweet known as baci di dama. It is said that this sugary confection so tempted the donkey on which Saint Lucy rode that he stopped at every house where the confection had been placed outside. In place of the sweets, he left gifts for children.

✟ The gift of sight is much more meaningful than just being able to see. A wise person, though blind, sees through confusion, deception, manipulation, and trickery. Spend a few moments thinking or writing about what the phrase "seeing the light" means to you. Think of moments in your life when you were blind and remember how well you saw or understood a situation after your blinders were removed.

✛ If you were to promise, as Saint Lucy did, your body and mind to Christ, what would you have to give up? What would you hope to get in return? What if the Lord blessed you with the special gift of spiritual sight and insight? How would you use these gifts for the highest good of others? If you had these gifts and could impart them to others, would you? Why or why not? Ask these questions and let your thoughts go where the answers take you.

✛ Choose a biblical word that you feel is potent with meaning. Write the word on a piece of paper and, without consciously picking and choosing, editing or refining, write all the associations that come to you around that word. When your paper is filled with these new words, use them all in a sacred prayer or poem. Then read this poem or prayer when you have time to meditate. Let the words lead your thoughts inward. Fill a journal with poems and prayers you create in this way.

AFFIRMATIONS

I seek happiness in solace with the Lord.

I give up the pleasures of the material world.

I will become one of God's faithful, holding high the lamp of truth to guide myself and others safely through the pitfalls of life.

Prayer to Saint Lucy

O Saint Lucy, who stood firm in your convictions even as unwelcome advances from an unwanted suitor threatened your hope for a peaceful, prayerful life in Christ, pray for us whose faith needs deepening that we may not be uprooted from our convictions. Pray to our Lord with us and for us that we may walk in light and understanding on the path of Christian living and not be buffeted by the angry emotions or dark intentions of others who would try to dissuade us. Blessed virgin and martyr, mercifully grant that we who venerate your sacrifice may receive your intercession. Amen.

FORGIVE US OUR TRESPASSES AS WE FORGIVE THOSE WHO TRESPASS
AGAINST US. — FROM THE LORD'S PRAYER. MATTHEW 6:12

SAINT MARIA GORETTI

For many of us, it's one thing to forgive another's trespass—whether it's an insult, hurtful gossip, or an act of violence. It's quite another thing to find forgiveness in our hearts when the act is murder. That is what makes young Saint Maria Goretti's gift of forgiveness so remarkable. She forgave her murderer moments before dying, and in so doing served as the supreme example of the Lord's teaching.

Maria, or Mariettas, as she was often called, was born in 1890 in a village in Italy. Her parents, Luigi Goretti and Assunta Carlini, had six children, including Maria. Shortly after Luigi, a farm laborer, moved the family to Ferriere di Conca, located near Nettuno in the Roman Campagna, he contracted malaria and died. Assunta had to work, doing whatever she could to feed her children. Times were tough. During the family's struggle to survive, young Maria was cheerful and encouraging, appreciating her mother's efforts.

In 1902, on a hot summer afternoon while her mother was away working, 11-year-old Maria was mending a shirt and minding her baby sister when a neighbor arrived, an 18-year-old boy named Alessandro Serenelli. He ran upstairs in the cottage and tried to lure Maria into a bedroom. Maria refused. Alessandro physically overpowered her and pulled her into the room, shutting the door behind them.

Maria struggled and, in spite of his strangulation hold, somehow managed to declare she would rather die than submit. Alessandro tore at her dress and began stabbing her with a dagger. Ultimately, perhaps to silence her cries, he plunged the dagger into her back and left her for dead.

Someone summoned an ambulance that transported Maria to a local hospital, but the doctors determined that it was unlikely she would live. During the ensuing hours, Maria confessed that she had feared the boy prior to the attack but had not spoken out because she didn't want to make trouble for him with his family. She worried about where her mother would sleep as she sat vigil for her daughter, and finally, Maria forgave Alessandro and said it was her wish that he could be with her in paradise. Within 24 hours of her attack, Maria was dead.

Lived–A.D. 1890–1902
Martyred–Virgin martyr
Beatified–1947
Canonized–1950 as a martyr for chastity
Feast day–July 6
Patron saint of rape victims, girls, and Catholic youth

Convicted of murder, Alessandro was unrepentant for the first eight years of his 30-year sentence—until he experienced a profound dream. In it, Maria offered him the flowers she was gathering. The experience so changed Alessandro that upon being released after serving 27 years, he went straight to Maria's mother and asked her forgiveness.

After Maria's death, many people revered her memory, and on April 27, 1947, she was declared blessed by Pope Pius XII. Three years later, Pope Pius XII canonized Maria Goretti in front of a crowd of more than 250,000 people. Some sources say Alessandro was there and witnessed the event. Maria's remains are kept in Our Lady of Grace church in Nettuno. ✛

WAYS TO HONOR AND INVOKE THE BLESSINGS OF SAINT MARIA GORETTI

✛ Find quiet time to do some soul searching. Is there an old grudge against someone that you haven't been able to release? Work to let it go and to forgive that trespass. Pray the Lord's Prayer and ask God to help you learn to forgive. Seek Saint Maria Goretti's intercession on your behalf.

✛ Gather some flowers and offer them to someone who is hurting.

✛ Plant some flower seeds in a pot half-filled with soil. Write down memories of old hurts and grudges, cut them to shreds, and put the bits in with the flower seed. Add more soil and water. As the flowers grow, they will be a reminder that beautiful things come of forgiveness.

✛ Smile as though the Lord himself were using your mouth and eyes to greet others with a smile. Be a generous giver of that gift. Engage the poor hearts of the world with a sincere and loving smile.

✣ Do a meditation on peace. Let your mind move from violence to peace. Think of Saint Maria Goretti, whose life was cut short in a single act of violence. Then consider how the Lord filled her spirit with so much love and peace that she could forgive her murderer. Allow your thoughts to dwell upon the "hot" spots of the world where violence flares without warning. Mentally send peaceful thoughts to the people of those places. Feel the peaceful waters of the Lord washing over that place, cooling tempers and calming hearts.

AFFIRMATIONS

I release the hurts, betrayals, and grudges that fetter my heart.

I forgive as Christ forgives.

I will do battle with my enemies using the weapon of love.

Through love, I will be victorious in all avenues of my life.

✣✣✣✣✣✣✣✣✣✣✣✣✣✣✣✣✣✣✣✣✣✣✣

Novena to Saint Maria Goretti

Saint Maria Goretti, strengthened by God's grace, you did not hesitate, even at the age of 11, to sacrifice life itself to defend your virginal purity. Look graciously on the unhappy human race that has strayed far from the path of eternal salvation. Teach us all, and especially our youth, the courage and promptness that will help us avoid anything that could offend Jesus. Obtain for me a great horror of sin so that I may live a holy life on earth and win eternal glory in heaven. Please intercede for me in obtaining the favor I now ask (mention your request). *Amen.*

Recite this novena nine times in a row for nine days in a row.

— CALAMARI AND DIPASQUA, 1999

✣✣✣✣✣✣✣✣✣✣✣✣✣✣✣✣✣✣✣✣✣✣✣

THEN WERE THERE BROUGHT UNTO HIM LITTLE CHILDREN, THAT
HE SHOULD PUT HIS HANDS ON THEM, AND PRAY: AND THE DISCIPLES
REBUKED THEM. BUT JESUS SAID, SUFFER LITTLE CHILDREN,
AND FORBID THEM NOT, TO COME UNTO ME:
FOR OF SUCH IS THE KINGDOM OF HEAVEN.

— MATTHEW 19: 13–14

SAINT MARTIN DE PORRES

Have you ever been on vacation to a new city and, with your money belt cinched securely to your waist, set out to explore the environs, only to be approached by a young panhandler or street urchin asking for loose change? Increasingly, U.S. cities like San Francisco, Los Angeles, and New York are witnessing a growing number of homeless people living on the streets. Many are teens, some even as young as 11 or 12. We don't like to see it, but there it is: kids who are unwanted, unloved, and neglected, lacking basic necessities and often exploited right here on the streets of the richest country of the world. How could it happen? What can be done?

These social issues are not new and still do not have easy answers. Some 500 years ago, Martin de Porres, a saint from Lima, Peru, suffered racial intolerance and the insults of others because he was the mixed-race, illegitimate son of a white Spanish nobleman. Martin used to give away his mother's precious few pennies to those living on the streets and in desperate need. He grew up to become a profoundly spiritual person who cared for people in need regardless of their race or color. He has been called a patron of social justice and an apostle of charity, but he called himself a "mulatto dog."

He was born in Lima in 1579. His father, John de Porres, was a Spanish knight of the Order of Alcantara, and his mother, Anna Velasquez, was a free black woman from Panama. Martin had a dark complexion and his mother's features, none of which pleased John, who would have preferred that his son have whiter skin. Nevertheless, John claimed the boy as his.

John had a government post, and his work required him to live in Guayaquil, Ecuador, while Anna, Martin, and Joan (Martin's younger sister) stayed in Lima. John visited the family whenever he could. For about a four-year period early in Martin's life, the boy and his sister Joan lived with their father in Ecuador, until John de Porres had to leave that country to govern Panama. Still, John gave Anna enough money to enable Martin to complete his education and learn a trade.

At the age of 12, Martin chose to become a barber-surgeon-pharmacist-doctor (the combination of professions was not uncommon in that era) and apprenticed in the shop of Marcel de Rivero. Martin was attentive and competent, and before long Marcel was leaving the shop in Martin's hands. In time, clients began to prefer Martin's skills to Marcel's. That meant that Martin could have become financially

Lived–A.D. 1579–1639
Beatified–1837
Canonized–1962
Feast day–November 3
Special title–Apostle of Charity
Patron saint of race relations, social justice, hairdressers, and African-Americans

successful. However, he had such a charitable soul that he often refused payment, especially from the poor.

He worked during the day and visited churches on the way to work and also on the way home. Then he shut himself up in his room to pray through the night and do spiritual reading. Needing light to read, he begged candle stubs from the owner of Ventura de Luna, the house where he lived. Curious, the owner spied on him at night through the keyhole in the door to his room. She was amazed to see Martin kneeling in prayer with his arms outstretched like Jesus' on the cross.

Martin often experienced visions and ecstasies while he prayed, and the owner of the house told her friends, who told others. Soon the entire town was aware of the practices of this deeply spiritual young man.

Martin joined the Dominicans, not as a brother but as a lay helper. His job was washing toilets and other menial tasks like sweeping corridors and cells. When Martin's father discovered this, he used all his influence to get his son accepted as a lay brother or cleric. Martin protested, saying that he had chosen to be an abject and would not change his mind.

During his time at the monastery, Martin worked as gardener, barber, and counselor while at the same time caring for those who suffered from all manner of illnesses, including the plague. He showed a gentle kindness toward animals, including rats and other vermin, and extended a loving spirit of acceptance and understanding toward all humans.

Martin eventually became a lay brother of the Dominicans and established an orphanage and other charitable institutions in Lima. He also cared for slaves from Africa who were brought into Peru. Many miracles were attributed to him during his lifetime, including one when he was asked to lay his hand upon the chest of the Felician de Vega, who was en route to the place where he was to be named archbishop of Mexico. As a result of Martin's ministration, de Vega's fever and pain promptly disappeared.

Martin de Porres spent over 50 years ministering to the citizens of Lima and the Dominican brethren. He died in 1639 from a fever. Many noblemen and prelates of the church served as his pallbearers. ✛

And everyone that hath forsaken houses, or brethren, or sisters, or father, or mother, or lands, for my name's sake, shall receive a hundredfold, and shall inherit everlasting life.

— MATTHEW 19:2

WAYS TO HONOR AND INVOKE THE BLESSINGS OF SAINT MARTIN DE PORRES

✝ Get involved in social justice issues as they pertain to the poor, homeless, and especially street kids. Make your life count by making a difference in their lives.

✝ Meditate on the seven gifts of the Holy Spirit: wisdom, understanding, counsel, knowledge, piety, holy fear, and fortitude. Heed God's instructions and consecrate your heart each day to God, asking for his help in all things you wish to achieve.

✝ Create a Saint Martin de Porres medal using polymer clay and a photocopy of his image. Knead the clay and roll it out to desired thickness. Transfer the photocopied image by gently burnishing it into the clay. Cut the clay and fit it into a small, metal aspirin box; then bake according to the clay manufacturer's instructions. Paint the box and glue a pin or clip on the back. Have the medal blessed by a priest.

Prayer to Saint Martin de Porres

Blessed Saint Martin de Porres, whose own suffering at the hands of racially intolerant people opened your heart to our Lord, who lifted you up to a place of honor in heaven, pray for us that we might learn to see all human beings as God's wondrous creatures and not favor one race or color over another. As we seek God's blessings to enable us to be especially loving and helpful to those children in our society and world who feel unloved, unwanted, and victimized, we ask for your intercessory prayers. Pray with us and for us to our Lord Jesus Christ for their protection as well as for our own souls that we may aspire to the virtues you perfected: humility and love for your brethren and for the poor and needy. May God open our hearts and strengthen our minds that we will be better able to solve society's problems as they relate to the issues of homelessness, racial intolerance, and forgotten children. Amen.

BUT MARY STOOD WITHOUT AT THE SEPULCHER WEEPING: AND AS SHE
WEPT SHE STOOPED DOWN AND LOOKED INTO THE SEPULCHER, AND
SEETH TWO ANGELS IN WHITE, SITTING, THE ONE AT THE HEAD AND THE
OTHER AT THE FEET, WHERE THE BODY OF JESUS HAD LAIN. AND THEY
SAY UNTO HER, WOMAN, WHY WEEPEST THOU?

— JOHN 20:11–13

SAINT MARY MAGDALENE

A penitent is someone who feels and exhibits remorse for his or her sins. Penitentiaries are full of people who have sinned. Sinning is easy. Asking forgiveness, feeling contrition, and abstaining from sin is difficult, but it is what we must do if we are to live our lives in a way that is pleasing to God.

An example of one of the Bible's best-known penitents was a woman named Mary Magdalene. After repenting and being healed by Jesus, she became one of his most beloved followers. It is not by accident, but rather symbolic of the times in which she lived, that all 12 of Jesus' apostles were men.

"Woman," the angels said, and theirs were the first words Mary heard that morning inside Jesus' empty tomb. Mary Magdalene had made her way to the tomb in the soft light of breaking day the morning after the crucifixion. She stood in disbelief, looking, yet not seeing the body of Jesus. She felt shaken to her core, for she was deeply grieving. This was Jesus, her master, the one she loved most in the world, whose body had disappeared. She had come to the tomb with spices and ointment.

Turning and seeing, perhaps through eyes swimming with tears, a man standing near her, Mary heard him ask the same question.

"Woman, why weepest thou? Whom seeketh thou?"

— JOHN 22:15

Thinking he was a gardener, she pleaded with him to tell her where they might have taken Jesus. In that powerful moment in the half-light of dawn, he spoke her name: "Mary." Her heart must have quickened with joy.

She turned herself, and saith unto him, Rabboni, which is to say, Master.

— JOHN 22:16

On that day, Mary Magdalene was blessed among women to be the first to see the risen Christ. To her, Jesus gave the task of telling the others. She witnessed his new form, not the physical, earthly body of the man whom she called master, but his eternal form. Later, others would see him also and observe where the nails and sword had pierced his body. But it was Mary who received this momentous and significant blessing of being the first to see the risen Lord and to be commanded by him to proclaim it.

Lived–First century
Feast day–July 22
Patron saint of repentant sinners, the contemplative life, hairdressers, and perfume makers

Jesus saith unto her, Touch me not: for I am not yet ascended to my Father: but go to my brethren, and say unto them, I ascend unto my Father and your Father and to my God and your God. Mary Magdalene came and told the disciples that she had seen the Lord, and that he had spoken these things unto her.

— JOHN 22:17–18

Mary came from the town of Magdala and may have been an important person in that community. However, she suffered from possession by seven devils, which Jesus cast out, miraculously curing her. Mary was exceedingly grateful. Her faith was nothing less than monumental, her belief unstoppable, and her love unshakable.

She has been depicted in art as a beautiful and spiritual woman, but also as a sinner seeking forgiveness. She often is pictured holding a pot of ointment. Some famous paintings of her include El Greco's *Repentant Magdalen*, Giotto's *Crucifixion*, and Titian's *Noli Me Tangere*, which means "Do not touch me," the words Christ spoke to Mary Magdalene.

Mary may have been the first contemplative, and she followed the Lord's commandments faithfully. She was not afraid to be with him at the cross, standing stoically beneath it with the Lord's mother, the disciples, and others who loved him and followed his teachings. And she helped prepare the spices and ointments for anointing his body.

Little else is known about Mary. She was highly venerated in England, with nearly 200 ancient churches established in her name. Both Oxford and Cambridge have a college dedicated to her. Reputedly, she is buried at Saint Maximin in France. ✟

✢ Make a small triptych—three small wooden panels hinged together so that they open and close—and paint or glue an image of Jesus in the center, with his mother and Mary Magdalene each on one outer panel. Make it beautiful, as all holy things must be. Take this small devotional altar with you to places in nature where you can open it and begin prayerful meditation, or look at it while you say the rosary. Have your priest bless it.

✢ In the spring, before Easter, plant some impatiens, also called the touch-me-not plant. Let them remind you of the Lord's words after his resurrection.

✢ Buy some scented oil or make a mixture of scents that you find pleasing. Be sure to add some myrrh in honor of Mary Magdalene's mixing of spices and ointments for our Lord. Put a drop on each of your wrists as you prepare to pray the rosary. Once this becomes a habit, you will always associate that particular scent with the holy activity of prayer.

✢ Set aside one hour each week to spend in deep contemplation of the Passion of Christ. Pray for the intercession of Saint Mary Magdalene, asking that your restless mind become calm and quiet so that you can plunge ever deeper into a meditative state. Invite the Lord to come, to be with you.

Prayer to Saint Mary Magdalene

Blessed Saint Mary Magdalene, who sought our Lord in the sepulcher and to whom Jesus saw favor to reveal himself as the risen Christ, help us strengthen our commitment to and unquestioning faith in God, our Father, at all times, but especially when we are grieving for a loved one. Glorious Saint Mary Magdalene, show us how to light the match of devotion to ignite our hearts with that burning love you bore for Jesus. We ask you to pray for us and with us to Lord Jesus Christ that we may be absolved of our sins and that we may be fit to become beacons for other sinners who are lost and seeking his light. We will be ever mindful and grateful to you, blessed Saint Mary Magdalene, for hearing our petitions and interceding on our behalf to our Lord. Amen.

HAIL MARY, FULL OF GRACE, THE LORD IS WITH THEE; BLESSED ART THOU
AMONG WOMEN, AND BLESSED IS THE FRUIT OF THY WOMB, JESUS.
HOLY MARY, MOTHER OF GOD, PRAY FOR US SINNERS, NOW AND AT THE
HOUR OF OUR DEATH. AMEN.

— THE HAIL MARY PRAYER

MARY, MOTHER OF GOD

Learning how to be a good parent is one of life's most difficult jobs. It is also one of the most important. How, then, might a woman approach this role if she knew she would be the mother of God? We can only marvel at how that young Nazarene girl, destined for divine motherhood, accomplished what must have been for her the most difficult and important of jobs. Yet she did it with purity, humility, and obedience.

The mother of Jesus is known by countless names and titles, but perhaps the most beautiful is Mother of God (Greek: *Theotokos* or God-bearer). She is also the mother of all saints. Revered all over the world, Mary embodies the most majestic and perfect image of womanhood. She is called by some the second "Eve" and the spiritual mother of all.

While mothers and the motherless alike seek her merciful compassion and loving

Lived—First Century
Commemoration days—January 1, Mary, Mother of God; January 8, Our Lady of Prompt Succor; February 11, Our Lady of Lourdes; March 25, The Annunciation; May 13 (first day of apparition), Our Lady of Fatima; June 27, Our Lady of Perpetual Help; July 16, Our Lady of Mount Carmel; August 15, The Assumption; September 8, The Nativity of the Virgin Mary; September 15, Our Lady of Sorrows; December 8, Immaculate Conception, Our Lady of the Miraculous Medal; December 12, Our Lady of Guadalupe
Patron saint of many countries, including the United States, and also of virgins and Louisiana

comfort, other believers are attracted to Mary because of countless miracles attributed to her throughout time and in many different places in the world. These faithful make pilgrimages, sometimes even risking their own lives, to seek the intercession of the Mother of God on their behalf for healing, protection, support in their endeavors, strength, relief from suffering, help with afflictions, and solace from grief. For how could our Lord refuse a petition from his mother, our mother?

Beyond the major events recorded in the early Gospels regarding Mary's life—namely, the annunciation, the immaculate conception, the visitation, the birth of Jesus, and the assumption—little else is known. Born to Ann and Joachim, a Jewish couple past their childbearing years, Mary was their miracle child and God's answer to their prayers. The name Mary derives from the Hebrew word Marah (meaning myrrh) or from Miryam (meaning bitter). Mary's life had the sweetness of the scent of myrrh but also the bitterness of sorrow.

Mary was betrothed to the carpenter Joseph, of the house of David. She was not yet married when the angel Gabriel appeared to her saying, "Hail, thou that art highly favored, the Lord is with thee!" (Luke 1:28)

Mary may have been filled with fear and apprehension when the angel explained how, through the power of the Holy Spirit, she would conceive and bear a child that she was to call Jesus.

Mary's cousin Elizabeth, middle aged and previously barren, was miraculously six month's pregnant with John the Baptist when Mary visited her to share the good news. During the visit with Elizabeth, Mary offered a prayer of praise and exultation to God, a prayer now known as the Magnificat.

In the months and years that followed, Mary was to experience the pains of childbirth and the challenges of raising her child, the only begotten Son of God. She endured the three-day loss of her child, who was found talking with learned men in the temple; endured widowhood; suffered the gradual breaking of human ties between mother and son; and witnessed the murder of Jesus before her eyes.

There is no record of her ever refusing to accept any part of God's plan for her life. *Mater Delorosa*, or Mother of Sorrows, is another of Mary's titles, for surely, was not her path filled with sorrow? And yet, through all the trials and tribulations, Mary quietly bore it all, never wavering in her trust and her faith in God.

Through the centuries, whenever a baptismal name was to be chosen for a child, Mary's hallowed name in its myriad of cultural renderings often was invoked and continues to be a popular choice. Today, the teenage girl who once lived a quiet and obscure life is recognized and venerated as not only the most important woman in history but also as the ultimate example of motherhood. ✛

WAYS TO HONOR AND INVOKE THE BLESSINGS OF MARY

✛ Make a pilgrimage to one of the principle Marion shrines, such as Chartres, France, where Mary's tunic is kept, or to places where she has appeared, including Mount Carmel, Israel (first chapel dedicated to the Madonna); Czestochowa, Poland; Lourdes, France; Loreto, Italy; Knock, Ireland; Medjugorje, Herzegovina; Fatima, Portugal; and Guadalupe, Mexico, among others. In the United States, choose from the National Shrine of the Immaculate Conception, Washington, D.C.; Grotto of the Redemption, West Bend, Iowa; Mary, Queen of the Universe Shrine, Orlando, Florida; National Shrine of Our Lady of Czestochowa, Doylestown, Pennsylvania; National Shrine of the Miraculous Medal, Perryville, Missouri; Our Lady of the Snows, Bellville, Illinois; and Our Lady of Prompt Succor, New Orleans, to name a few.

✛ Purchase or create a small altar bell. Ring it reverently before beginning prayers and meditations on Mary.

✛ Spend part or all of a Saturday (Mary's day, whereas Sunday is regarded as devoted to Jesus) creating spiritual art to honor Mary—make a cigar-box shrine; paint her image in watercolor, acrylics, or oils; sew a wall quilt depicting an important moment in her life; string beads to make a chaplet or rosary, so named after *Rosa Mystica*, or Mystical Rose, one of Mary's popular titles.

✛ Celebrate Mother's Day in devotional activity honoring Mary. Plant a rose bush and install a statue of Mary in a garden. Whenever you visit the garden, shower the statue with rose petals and pray the Hail Mary or the entire rosary.

✛ Read, pray, and contemplate one or more of the four ancient prayers to Mary—Hail Mary, Hail Holy Queen, Memorare, and The Angelus.

✛ Listen to music written to venerate her glory and holiness, such as the compact disc titled *La bele Marie, Songs to the Virgin from 13th-Century France*, music performed by Anonymous 4 (www.harmoniamundi.com).

✛ On one or more of Mary's feast days, make soul cakes or doughnuts, so named because of their circular form that symbolizes the circle of life.

✛ Prayerfully walk the stations of the cross in your church. It has been said that Mary walked the *via dolorosa* (the way of sorrow, or the way of the cross) daily.

Novena to Mother of God

I greet you, ever-blessed Virgin, Mother of God, throne of grace, miracle of almighty power! I greet you, sanctuary of the Most Holy Trinity and Queen of the Universe, Mother of mercy and refuge of sinners!

Most loving Mother, attracted by your beauty and sweetness, and by your tender compassion, I confidently turn to you, and beg of you to obtain for me of your dear Son the favor I request in this novena: (mention your request).

Obtain for me also, Queen of Heaven, the most lively contrition for my many sins and the grace to imitate closely those virtues which you practiced so faithfully, especially humility, purity, and obedience. Above all, I beg you to be my mother and protectress, to receive me into the number of your devoted children, and to guide me from your high throne of glory.

Do not reject my petitions, Mother of mercy!

Have pity on me and do not abandon me during life or at the moment of my death.

Daughter of the Eternal Father, Mother of the Eternal Son, Spouse of the Holy Spirit, Temple of the Adorable Trinity, pray for me. Immaculate and tender Heart of Mary, refuge of the needy and hope of sinners, filled with the most lively respect, love, and gratitude, I devote myself forever to your service, and I offer you my heart with all that I am and all that is mine.

Accept this offering, sweet Queen of Heaven and Earth, and obtain for me of your dear Son, Jesus Christ, the favors I ask through your intercession in this novena. Obtain for me also a generous, constant love of God, perfect submission to his holy will, the true spirit of a Christian, and the grace of final perseverance. Amen.

Recite this novena nine times in a row for nine days in a row.

— LOVASIK, 2000

AND JESUS, WALKING BY THE SEA OF GALILEE, SAW TWO BRETHREN,
SIMON CALLED PETER, AND ANDREW HIS BROTHER, CASTING A NET
INTO THE SEA; FOR THEY WERE FISHERS. AND HE SAITH UNTO THEM,
"FOLLOW ME, AND I WILL MAKE YOU FISHERS OF MEN." AND THEY
STRAIGHTWAY LEFT THEIR NETS, AND FOLLOWED HIM.

— MATTHEW 4:18–20

SAINT MATTHEW

If the Lord appeared to you in the next instant and asked you to leave everything and follow him, would you be ready? What would you have to give up in the way of earthly attachments, possessions, lifestyle choices, habits, and relationships? You don't have all day to answer him. What will you say? Saint Matthew (who was also called Levi) said yes to Jesus.

And after these things he went forth, and saw a publican named Levi, sitting at the receipt of custom: and he said unto him, Follow me.

And he left all, rose up, and followed him.

— LUKE 5:27–28

Before he became one of the 12 apostles and an evangelist, Matthew was a tax collector working for the Romans, though he was himself a Jew. Not surprisingly, he is commonly associated with the symbol of three purses. These represent his profession before he met and was called to serve the Lord.

Perhaps because he was used to dealing with money, records, and minute details, his Gospel is written in a style that is direct and succinct. In that Gospel, he logically lays out the paternal genealogy of the Lord's earthly family. After setting forth the genealogy, Matthew includes a mathematical summary of the breakdown of generations within each era by writing, "So all the generations from Abraham to David are fourteen generations; and from David until the carrying away into Babylon are fourteen generations, and from the carrying away into Babylon unto Christ are fourteen generations." (Matthew 1:17)

Matthew's clear and concise descriptions of the important events in the life of Jesus make his Gospel an all-time favorite. From the verses in the first few chapters where he details Christ's conception, birth, and escape to Egypt to avoid the persecution of Herod, to the passion and the details of Jesus' resurrection in the twenty-eighth chapter, Matthew's storytelling has inspired millions of readers seeking the truth, wisdom, and words of Jesus. In the Gospel of Matthew, we learn the horrifying details of our Lord's death.

Lived–First century
Feast day–September 21
Patron saint of bankers, tax collectors, security guards, customs officials, moneychangers, watchmen, and accountants

*And when they had platted a crown of
thorns, they put it upon his head, and a reed
in his right hand: and they bowed the knee
before him, and mocked him, saying, Hail,
King of the Jews! And they spit upon him,
and took the reed, and smote him on the
head. And after they had mocked him, they
took the robe off from him, and put his own
raiment on him, and led him away to crucify
him.*

— MATTHEW 27:29–31

Further into the story of the passion,
Matthew reveals that Pilate's soldiers gave
Jesus a bitter drink meant to torment him
even more.

*They gave him vinegar to drink, mingled
with gall: and when he tasted thereof, he
would not drink. And they crucified him, and
parted his garments, casting lots: that it might
be fulfilled which was spoken by the prophet;
They parted my garments among them and
upon my vesture did they cast lots. And sitting down, they watched him there: And set
up over his head his accusation written, THIS
IS THE KING OF THE JEWS.*

— MATTHEW 27:34–37

The Gospel of Matthew closes with some
of the most beautiful words in the Bible—
these spoken by Jesus:

*"Go ye therefore and teach all nations, bap-
tizing them in the name of the Father, and
of the Son, and of the Holy Ghost; teaching
them to observe all things whatsoever I have
commanded you: and lo, I am with you
always, even unto the end of the world."*

— MATTHEW 28:19–20

After the resurrection of Christ, not much
else is known about where Matthew went
and what he did. Some say he preached in
Judea, while others say he journeyed
among lands in the Middle East and to
destinations even further east. Matthew was
following the counsel of Jesus to take God's
word to the people of all lands.

*Sanctify them through thy truth: thy word is
truth. As thou hast sent me into the world,
even so have I also sent them into the world.*

— JOHN 17:17–18

One religious document suggests that
Matthew was martyred evangelizing in
Ethiopia, while another indicates Persia.
Several places claim to have his relics,
including Salerno, France, and Britanny. He
is the patron saint of the city of Salerno
and of the diocese as well. In art, Matthew
is often shown with a money-box, account
books, and glasses or writing tools. ✣

✝ Keep a jar in your house and designate it the bank for loose change. Decorate it with a holy image of Saint Matthew. When the jar is full, roll the coins in wrappers and donate the money to causes that help the poor, sick, and needy.

✝ Teach your children how to save money both for themselves and for the poor so that they may learn to be charitable as they grow and mature.

✝ Volunteer at a soup kitchen.

✝ Seek out a food bank and see how you can help. Perhaps you can spearhead a food drive in your neighborhood or at your children's school.

Prayer to Saint Matthew

O Saint Matthew, beloved disciple of Jesus who did not falter or make excuses when the Lord called, help me to be so assured and strong in my resolve that I, too, can leave everything behind for Jesus. Help me to embrace my path to the Lord with utmost clarity, and open my heart to all the possibilities he places there. Glorious Saint Matthew, help me always to remember that whatsoever Jesus asks us to give up, he replaces a hundredfold. Pray for me and with me to our Lord, that I will not be afraid to replace old habits with new ones pleasing to him. Show me how not to fear being poor. Show me how not to be greedy and long for riches. Show me how to love all, without concern about whether I'm loved back. Let me not be attached to the fruits of my labor or take credit for those things I do not deserve. Blessed Saint Matthew, help me empty myself of the heavy emotional baggage that weighs me down that I may feel light and free and ready to serve as our Lord Jesus Christ draws me to him. Amen.

GREATER LOVE HAS NO MAN THAN THIS,
THAT A MAN LAY DOWN HIS LIFE FOR HIS FRIENDS.

— JOHN 15:13

SAINT MAXIMILIAN MARIA KOLBE

W hat is the greatest sacrifice you've had to make in your life? Unless you are a police officer or a soldier serving in a branch of the military, you are seldom called to make the ultimate sacrifice—to lay down your life for another. More often, that's the stuff of movies and dramatic storytelling. But would you? Could you? What if you had been given the choice of preserving your purity or dying as a martyr by giving up your life so another might live? Which would you choose? Saint Maximilian Kolbe, a modern saint, chose both.

He was born on January 7, 1894 in the village of Pabianice, Poland, to Julius Kolbe, a textile factory worker, and his wife Maria, a devout Catholic and hard-working mother. The family had a little altar behind one of the wardrobes in their home. This is where young Raymond went one day after his mother chastised him for his behavior and asked, perhaps rhetorically, what would ever become of him.

In fact, Raymond frequently disappeared to spend time at the altar. One day he admitted to his mother that her question had so worried him that he'd gone to the altar to ask the Mother of God. The Blessed

Mother appeared to him with a white crown in one hand and a red crown in the other. She asked Raymond which he wanted: a life of purity that she would preserve for him or death as a martyr. He chose both. He told his mother that "Our Lady" smiled and disappeared.

In 1907, the Franciscans came to Pabianice to inspire young villagers and talk to them about the vocation of a religious life. Soon, Raymond was accepted into the Franciscan minor seminary in L'viv, which was in an Austrian province.

Raymond took temporary vows on September 11, 1911, but he still had doubts that tormented him. An abscess on his thumb that was miraculously healed with holy water from Lourdes helped strengthen his faith, and seven years later, Raymond took his perpetual vows and the religious name of Maximilian. In 1915, he received a doctorate of philosophy from Pontifical Gregorian University and, four years later, a doctorate in theology from Saint Bonaventure Theological Faculty.

In 1919, after his ordination, Maximilian was diagnosed with tuberculosis while in Rome. He suffered miserably after the First World War began. Many around him thought his death might come soon, releasing this man who, as a young boy, had purchased a statue of the Madonna for a kopek and had promised the Mother of God that he would fight for her. At last he would be in heaven, united with the

Lived—A.D. 1894–1941
Feast day—August 14
Beatified—1971
Canonized—1982
Patron saint of addicts, drug addiction, families, prisoners, and journalists

Immaculata he so loved. Death, however, was not to be. Fighting for the Immaculata was about to begin.

On October 16, 1917, Maximilian founded the Crusade of Mary Immaculate (Militia Immaculatae). Then, on April 28, 1918, he was ordained a priest. Only a year later, Maximilian was sent to Poland with the prognosis that he had only three months to live. He recovered, but could breathe with only one lung. Despite this handicap, Maximilian established a newspaper that was dedicated to Mary and called the *Knights of the Immaculata*, and the paper miraculously kept increasing in subscriptions until there were a million subscribers. He also built the religious community of Niepokalanów (the City of the Immaculate) as a place to house his lay brothers and to grow the newspaper venture.

Maximilian worked indefatigably despite his poor health. In 1930, he went to Japan and started the newspaper there. Five years later, he started producing a daily Catholic newspaper, *The Little Daily*. In 1936, he was called back to Poland to be the Guardian (or Superior) of Niepokalanów, the religious community he had built. In 1938, he oversaw the establishment of a radio station in Niepokalanów, and his brothers played the signature tune of the Lourdes hymn on the air.

Soon, the ominous sounds of Hitler's goose-stepping Wehrmacht could be heard as the army marched through Polish cities and towns. In Niepokalanów, German soldiers deported many of the town's inhabitants. When the Germans left, Maximilian wasted no time organizing shelter for 3,000 Polish refugees. There were roughly 2,000 Jews among them. In aligning himself with Jews, gypsies, and others despised by the Nazis, Maximilian invited their rancor. In 1941, he wrote in an edition of *The Knights of the Immaculata* that "beyond armies of occupation and hecatombs of extermination camps, there are two irreconcilable enemies in the depth of every soul: good and evil, sin and love." That was all the Gestapo needed. They moved in and arrested him.

He was sent to Lamsdorf, Germany, and on to a camp at Amtlitz. After a period of internment, he returned to Niepokalanów, only to be re-arrested. On May 28 of that year, he was sent to Auschwitz. When one of the other prisoners escaped and could not be found, 10 internees were selected to be executed through death by starvation in an airless, underground cell. One, a man named Franz Gajowniczek, had a wife and children. Grief-stricken, he cried out their names over and over. Maximilian asked the Nazi commandant to allow him, a Polish Catholic priest, to die in place of Franz Gajowniczek. It was agreed.

While waiting for death with his nine comrades, Maximilian prayed, recited psalms, and offered encouragement to his companions. He showed great compassion and tenderness toward all. When he was too weak to sing praises to Mary or speak, he whispered his prayers. Of the 10 put to death, Maximilian was the last to die. He had remained alive for two weeks without food or water. Reportedly, he was serene and placed his arm where it was needed in order to receive the lethal injection of carbolic acid that would kill him. The date was August 14, 1941. The Germans marked the hour of death at 12:30. Maximilian was 47 years old.

The body of the champion and servant of Mary that the Germans identified as prisoner number 16770 was placed in the crematorium the next day, which was the day of the Feast of the Assumption of Mary. He was beatified by Pope Paul VI in 1971 and on October 10, 1982 was canonized by Pope John Paul II and declared a martyred saint. ✙

WAYS TO HONOR AND INVOKE THE BLESSINGS OF SAINT MAXIMILIAN MARIA KOLBE

✙ Venerate Saint Maximilian Kolbe by purchasing and wearing the Miraculous Medal.

✙ Speak out when you see injustices, lies, and demeaning messages being disseminated, especially about the church, the Holy Father, or the teachings of Jesus. Pray to God through the intercession of the Immaculata and her son Jesus for guidance, and give help to others dealing with these kinds of situations.

✙ Make a pilgrimage someday to the village of Saint Maximilian Kolbe's birth, to Auschwitz, or to the U.S. Holocaust Museum.

✙ Give of yourself. Make a sacrifice, however large or small, for another. Do it out of love and not self-aggrandizement.

✙ Support the Franciscans.

Prayer to Saint Maximilian Kolbe

O Saint Maximilian Kolbe, my heart holds your memory in a tender place, and my thoughts are ever flowing toward you in gratitude not only for your bravery and meritorious act but also for your devotion to our Blessed Mother Mary. With your example of risking everything for the Immaculata and then dying for someone else, you showed me what depths unconditional love can reach. You exemplified the ultimate meaning of Jesus' message, showing what loving thy neighbor as thyself truly means. Blessed Saint Maximilian, pray for me and with me to our Lord Jesus Christ, the model of all martyrs, that I may cultivate that kind of love for all humankind regardless of race, color, gender, nationality, or beliefs. Amen.

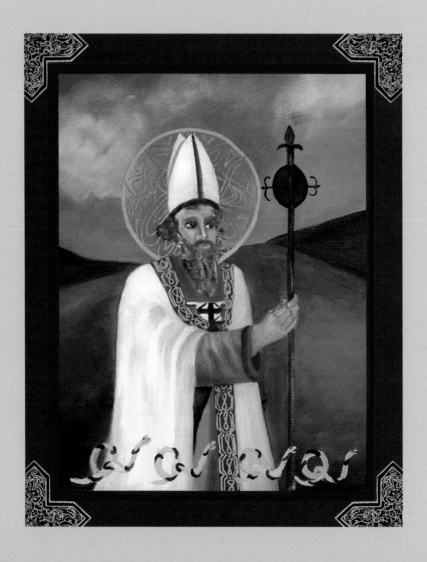

SAINT PATRICK

As we go about our daily activities, most of us don't think about who is the real doer in our lives, enabling us to accomplish all that we achieve through his grace. When we are complimented, we graciously accept and, perhaps, even feel a little proud. But the saints knew that all glory rightfully belongs to God, for without his loving grace, nothing is possible.

Down through the centuries, every saint has endeavored to praise and honor God's glory, each in his or her own way. Saint Patrick, the archbishop of Armagh and apostle of Ireland, was no exception. The exact location of his birthplace varies depending on which source you read, but Patrick himself admitted to being of Romano-British lineage.

He was the son of a deacon and municipal worker and the grandson of a priest. When he was 16, he was kidnapped by Irish pirates and imprisoned by Ireland's pagan inhabitants. While he endured much physical suffering, mentally he gave a great amount of thought to his condition. He came to believe that it was divine punishment for laxity in his religious practices. So it was that under these less than ideal circumstances, Patrick embraced a life of prayer.

Lived–a.d. 389–461
Feast day–March 17
Patron saint of Ireland, Nigeria, those who fear snakes, and engineers

After a half-dozen years, he had a vision telling him to get ready for a concerted effort to regain his freedom. While it is not known whether he escaped or was freed, Patrick made the grueling trip back to England, almost starving to death in the process. He was 22 years old when he was reunited with his family.

He embarked upon a rudimentary course of study to train as a priest. This included studying the Latin Bible, but the whole of his education was not the best, and for the rest of his days Patrick harbored regrets about his scholarly inadequacy. He spent time in Auxerre, France, studying religion under Saint Germanus, became a deacon, and eventually was ordained a bishop.

At some point, Patrick had a vision in a dream. A messenger brought him a packet of letters, and while reading one of them, he heard the voices of the Irish calling on him to return to their land. Initially, his superiors rejected his request. Once he was ordained as a bishop by Pope Celestine I, however, Patrick realized his dream.

He returned as the first bishop of Ireland sometime between A.D. 432 and 435. He established his see, or official jurisdiction, in Armagh in the northern part of the country, and from this base he set off on his missions to convert pagans, consecrate virgins, and ordain clergy. His efforts through the years profoundly influenced the Irish Catholic Church and infused it with enthusiasm and vibrancy. He founded many monasteries. He converted thousands, sometimes even entire tribes of people. Through it all, Patrick remained humble, giving all glory of accomplishment to God.

Legends say he drove the snakes out of Ireland, that he used the shamrock to explain the holy meaning of the Trinity, and that he alone converted almost the whole of Ireland to Christianity. These stories, as scholars point out, are likely more fiction than fact, but they grew to mythical proportions as Patrick's popularity swelled.

That Patrick faced danger daily is probably true. The words on his breastplate are known collectively as the "Deer Cry." The title comes from the story of an enemy king lying in wait to ambush Patrick and his men, not realizing they had become invisible. When Patrick's group passed by, all the king could see were deer. All he could hear were the words, "Christ with me, Christ before me…."

Today, people of many nations, cultures, and ethnic lineage celebrate Saint Patrick's Day on March 17 by participating in parades, wearing the color green, and making and eating foods such as corned beef and cabbage and Irish soda bread. They do these things in remembrance of a man who showed—through his prayerful life—how to perform one's work to magnify the blessings of God. One the most famous churches established in his name is Saint Patrick's Cathedral in New York. ✝

WAYS TO HONOR AND INVOKE THE BLESSINGS OF SAINT PATRICK

✝ Set aside six minutes—one minute for each year Saint Patrick was kept in slavery—before bed each night to thank God and give him glory for the gifts of grace, goodness, and accomplishment in your life.

✝ Buy or make a cross and adorn it with pique assiette mosaic (be sure to include some green china shards or glass to reflect the light) and hang it in your garden to honor this saint who had such great reverence for the pastoral landscape.

✝ Consider how, even in this modern age, you can emulate the example of Saint Patrick and make little changes in your life to lead a more prayerful existence.

✝ Read books about Saint Patrick's life, work, and teaching and consider visiting Ireland, especially the National Museum in Dublin, where Saint Patrick's bell and his tooth are enshrined.

✝ Put on a CD of soft Irish or Celtic music. Dance around the room to the beat of the music. Feel the musical patterns as rhythmic vibrations dancing through your body. Imagine your body's vibrations filling the room. When the music ends, sit quietly and feel the energy that still courses through you. Consider how, when you invite the Lord to come, his divine energy fills you like music throbbing in every muscle.

✛ Find a beautiful picture of Ireland or Saint Patrick. Use the visual image as a point of focus to enter a period of contemplation about Saint Patrick's life. What fears might he have felt during the six years he was enslaved by Irish pirates? He spent many of those years in prayer. What do you suppose he might have prayed about? What parallels might his life have to our modern lives?

✛ Saint Patrick received a message in a dream calling him back to Ireland, where he gave his life for the work of the Lord. What dream messages have you received in your life that felt potent? Consider keeping a dream journal. Write down all your dreams and take a little time each day to ponder them and render interpretations. Consult dream dictionaries until you can recognize recurring symbols that have particular meaning for you.

Saint Patrick's Breastplate Prayer

I bind unto myself today
the power of God to hold and lead,
his eye to watch, his might to stay,
his ear to harken to my need:
the wisdom of my God to teach,
his hand to guide, his shield to ward;
the word of God to give me speech,
his heavenly host to be my guard.

Christ be with me, Christ before me,
Christ behind me, Christ deep within me,
Christ below me, Christ above me,
Christ at my right hand, Christ at my left hand,
Christ as I lie down, Christ as I arise,
Christ as I stand,
Christ in the heart of everyone who thinks of me,
Christ in the mouth of everyone who speaks to me,
Christ in every eye that sees me,
Christ in every ear that hears me.

— GLENSTAL ABBEY, 2001

BLESSED ARE THE POOR IN SPIRIT:
FOR THEIRS IS THE KINGDOM OF HEAVEN.

— MATTHEW 5:3

SAINT PETER

Are you a follower or a leader? Or are you a little of each? The answer might depend upon the circumstances. In some situations, you might choose to be in charge. In others, you might feel intimidated or fearful that you aren't as qualified as someone else to do the job. What if Christ were the one asking you to take a leadership position? Would it be easier or more difficult to say yes?

A man named Simeon found himself in just such a position. He was handpicked by Jesus for a new job and given a new name: Cephas (Peter, meaning rock). His new job was to be a fisher of men, and his new name would serve him well in his role as the first founding pillar that would support the living church.

Peter was a Galilean, born in Bethsaida near the Sea of Galilee. He was married and had a brother named Andrew; both men were fishermen. Of the two, Peter was perhaps the born leader. Among the group of professional fishermen, Peter served as the one in charge. During Christ's life on earth, Peter was singled out by Jesus for the predominant role of leader among his disciples and followers.

Peter's now famous declaration of faith, "Thou art the Christ, the Son of the Living God" (Matthew 16:16), placed him in a preeminent position to lead others and be a spokesman for the teachings of Jesus. Jesus told Peter that he would have the power to bind and to loose and that to him would be given the keys of heaven. Peter, considered a common, uneducated man, asked the Messiah many important questions. When Peter fulfilled Jesus' prediction that Peter would deny him three times before the cock crowed, the Lord prayed that Peter's faith would grow and be strengthened.

After Jesus was put to death and had risen, Peter took charge among the apostles. He led an assemblage of 120 people in prayer and drew lots to choose a successor to Judas. The choice lay between Barsabbas (also known as Joseph) and Matthias. The appointment went to Matthias.

Later, when the time for Pentecost had come, Peter stepped forth to counter accusations that the followers of Jesus were drunk when, in fact, they were filled with the Holy Spirit and were heard to be speaking in tongues. He challenged those assembled who had not yet accepted Jesus to repent and convert that they too might be filled with the Holy Spirit.

Lived–First century
Martyred–Circa A.D. 64
Feast day–June 29
Patron saint of Germany, longevity, Rome, fishermen, the church, and the papacy

It was Peter who worked the first miracle, healing a crippled man begging at the gate to the temple in Jerusalem, a place known as the Beautiful Gate. And it was Peter who, before the Sanhedrin, defended the apostles' right to teach the people, proclaim the resurrection of Jesus, and work miracles.

Then Peter, filled with the Holy Ghost, said unto them, Ye rulers of the people, and the elders of Israel, if we this day be examined of the good deed done to the impotent man, by what means he is made whole; Be it known unto you all, and to all the people of Israel, that by the name of Jesus Christ of Nazareth, whom ye crucified, whom God raised from the dead, even by him doth this man stand here before you whole.

— ACTS 4:8–10

In yet another example of his leadership and organizational skills, Peter admitted Gentiles into the church, and he also established the church procedures that govern the succession of bishops. In fact, Saint Peter was an exceedingly important figure in the early church. Perhaps for this reason, Nero persecuted Peter in Rome, and ultimately Peter was crucified but, at his request and out of deference to his master, was placed with his head down so as to not occupy the same position as Jesus.

In third-century catacombs, graffiti in the lingua franca of the day contain messages of veneration to Peter. By the end of the second century or early third century, Peter had been identified as the first Bishop of Rome. He is buried beneath the Vatican.

In religious art, Peter is often depicted with icons such as keys (symbolizing the keys to heaven), a fish (he was a fisherman), and a rooster (for denying Jesus three times before the cock crowed). His name is a popular baptismal choice.

Saint Peter is also considered a universal saint, venerated by many as patron of the living church and the papacy as well as gatekeeper to heaven. ✠

WAYS TO HONOR AND INVOKE THE BLESSINGS OF SAINT PETER

✠ Take the lead. Do it with grace, as Peter did. Don't demand it. Ask God to be your co-leader. Whether it's bingo night at the church, a summer fundraiser festival, or a spring or autumn food drive, prepare, plan, and do it right—with foresight, 100 percent effort, and humility.

✠ Affirm Peter's statement to Jesus daily: "Thou art the Christ, the Son of the living God."

✠ Pray for the healing of the infirm who are suffering and waiting at the gates of death. Pray to God to have mercy on them and to fill them with the light and perfection of the Holy Spirit.

✠ Make the traditional almond cake on Saint Peter's feast day, or bake small votive breads for your celebration and dedicate them to Saint Peter, as believers do in Palazzolo Acreide in Sicily.

✠ Spend an hour during your week in Eucharistic adoration.

✠ Imagine the last hours of your life. If the Lord calls you, how quickly will you heed his call? How will you say your goodbyes to those in this life? Will you feel joy at the prospect of going "home" or sadness because of your attachments to things of this material world? Take some deep breaths, sit comfortably, and close your eyes. Feel the Holy Spirit intoning within you, calling you deeply inward. In this quiet, peaceful place, be still and await the Lord. After a while, mentally address your fears and your hopes. Let him know how you feel about the approach of the end of this life. Be honest. Take time to be still again and see what thoughts emerge around this topic. What does having a good death mean to you? Write your thoughts and conclusions in a sacred journal.

✠ If you have the good fortune of having access to a maze (for example, the one at Grace Cathedral in San Francisco), take some time off to walk the maze. People who have done so often report having had feelings of peace and healing during and after the walk. The maze ends at its center, much like the roads of life that we travel until we get to the end of our days. While walking the maze, ponder your life and ask yourself, have I lived in a meaningful way? What messages about my life will I be leaving behind for others?

Prayer to Saint Peter

O Blessed Saint Peter, who proclaimed to our Lord that "Thou art the Christ, the Son of the living God," and then denied him three times before the cock crowed, we appreciate those qualities that you possessed while in an earthly body. At times, doubt creeps into the lives of those of us who would also be leaders. You showed us by your example how to be human but also to be a bearer of light for the Holy Spirit. From your exalted place, pray with us and for us to our Lord Jesus that he might enable us to grow in moral character and leadership ability in order that we may better do his work on Earth. Blessed Saint Peter, we seek your intercession for God's blessings that we may be worthy vessels to hold his love, never doubting his love for us. Amen.

PARA SIEMPRE, PARA SIEMPRE (FOREVER, FOREVER).
— WORDS THAT TERESA, LESS THAN SEVEN YEARS OLD,
RECITED AS SHE TRIED TO IMAGINE THAT EXPANSE OF
TIME IN THE CONTEXT OF THE JOY OF HEAVEN

SAINT TERESA OF ÁVILA

How fortunate to come into the world with a loving mother and father. Not everyone is so lucky. When one or both parents die, it is common to feel as if you are all alone. However, if you turn to your heavenly mother and father and the saints as intercessors the way Saint Teresa of Ávila did, your experience may be very different.

Teresa Cepeda y Ahumada was born on March 28, 1515 to one of Ávila, Spain's wealthy merchant families. She grew up in a loving family and became an avid reader, thanks to her father's fine library. When Teresa was 14, her mother died. After her mother's death, Teresa asked the Mother of God to be her mother, and thereafter Teresa was educated by Augustinian nuns at a convent in Ávila.

Teresa fell ill about a year and a half later. During her recovery, she decided to pursue the life of a nun. At 20, she entered the Carmelite Convent of the Incarnation of Ávila, but once again she fell ill and had to leave the convent for treatment. This time her recuperation took nearly three years and left her crippled and unable to walk.

Undeterred, she prayed to Saint Joseph and recovered. When she returned to the convent, however, she found its community had grown to 140 nuns and that the rules about quiet and outside visitation had become lax.

She embraced instead the practice of mental prayer, only to give it up and then resume it again after her father died. In 1555, she experienced a deep, inner, mystical identification with the penitent Mary Magdalene and with Augustine of Hippo. The lives of these two saints, as well as Augustine's *Confessions*, were to greatly influence her thinking and beliefs.

Teresa longed for a place where she could practice a stricter, more severe form of Carmelite life. Eventually, she was allowed to start a new order: Saint Joseph of Ávila.

In the new convent with 13 nuns, Teresa was able at last to live a life of poverty and solitude. She put on a robe of coarse brown wool and donned sandals. She worked alongside everyone else—spinning, sweeping, and doing whatever needed to be done. The nuns abstained from eating meat and, together, held tightly to Teresa's vision of an austere life governed by a primitive rule. The convent's self-sufficiency was made possible by the hard manual labor of the nuns and by the alms given them.

Lived–A.D. 1515–1582
Canonized–1622
Feast day–October 15
Honors–Doctor of the Church, 1970 (she was the first woman)
Special titles–Spouse of Christ
Patron saint of headaches, those in need of grace, and Spain

Teresa worked actively in the 1560s, with the help of John of the Cross, to reform the Carmelite friars. On the eve of Saint Sebastian, January 19, 1572, as the nuns in the choir began to sing the "Salve Regina," Teresa experienced an ecstatic vision in which the blessed Virgin and a multitude of angels entered the church. The Virgin occupied the seat of the prioress and remained there through the singing of the prayer. Teresa heard Mary say that Teresa had been right to place Mary there and that Mary would be present for all her Son's praises and would present them to him. Many more visions and ecstatic states would visit Teresa in the coming years.

Teresa was ordered to write books describing her experiences, which she did. They included her examination of the spiritual life in *Life* (which she subtitled her "book of the Lord's favours"), *The Way of Perfection* (for the sisters of Saint Joseph's), and *The Interior Castle*. In these writings, we get a sense of Teresa and of her richly spiritual interior life of prayer. For her, prayer was the link that expressed love between a soul and God. And Teresa depended on God, her beloved spouse, for everything.

"I see truly, my Lord,
how little I am worth.
But now I am united with you
and have climbed to the top of that tower
which offers a view of all truth,
so if you stay with me,
I will achieve something.
But if instead you leave me,
then I will fall back where I was before,
on the way of wickedness."

—SAINT TERESA OF ÁVILA, 1997

Teresa went on to establish several convents. Her health failed again, and by the eve of Saint Francis, October 3, Teresa was so weak the nuns had to turn her from side to side. She seemed to be in a vigil with the Lord, at times singing and at other times praying or offering counsel to her nuns about keeping the rule of the order. That evening, she asked to be anointed and then told the priest that she would like to be buried in Alba.

The next day she seemed enraptured, her old face gloriously young and beautiful. At one point, when she saw Jesus in an ecstatic vision, she called out to him as her bridegroom and spouse, telling him that the hour had come and it was time for the two of them to go. At 9:00 that night, October 4, she breathed out a last soft sigh, and it was over.

She was buried in a simple brown habit that she had made. Afterwards, her nuns went often to the gravesite to pray. Many spoke of a sweet scent pervading the site.

Saint Teresa's body was exhumed nine months later and found to be incorrupt. Not only did the gravesite emit this scent, but also any object that had come in contact with Teresa's body, including towels, clothing, her dish, and, perhaps most especially, her cell. It is said that its windows had to be opened because the scent was so sweet and overpowering that those entering the cell developed headaches.

Many miracles were attributed to Teresa's intercession, and they continue to this day. Pope Paul V declared her blessed in 1614, and Pope Gregory XV canonized her in 1622. In art, she is often depicted with the icons of a dove over her head (symbolizing the Holy Spirit) and a fiery arrow. ☩

WAYS TO HONOR AND INVOKE THE BLESSINGS OF SAINT TERESA OF ÁVILA

☩ Give your fears, torments, and apprehensions over to God, as Saint Teresa did.

☩ Learn to love the silence. Saint Teresa knew that only through silence would she be able to hear the counsel of the Lord.

☩ Make good choices in reading material. Read the lives of the saints, Scripture, prayers, the liturgy of the church, and the writings of the saints and the popes.

☩ Practice the four forms of reverence, including family (toward the heads of your family), civil (toward community authorities), ecclesiastical (toward church authority), and religious (toward all humankind and that which God has created).

☩ Make or purchase the brown Carmelite scapular and wear it as an act of devotion to our Lord (and also to his mother Mary) so that in this act you are venerating his Discalced Carmelite saint, Teresa of Ávila. If you make it, be sure to have a priest bless it.

Prayer to Saint Teresa of Ávila

Beloved Saint Teresa of Ávila, Spouse of Christ, who sought heavenly love and protection from the Mother of God when your own mother died and from our Lord throughout your earthly life, we honor your example of a life lived virtuously for the glory of God. You overcame your faults, conquered Satan's temptations, and glorified God daily. Pray for us to our Lord and Savior that we may emulate your example of sanctity in our own earthly lives that we may be worthy of God's grace. We pray he will absolve us from our sins and draw up our souls and our bodies to him. Pray with us and for us to the Lord, asking him to forgive us our missteps and guide us firmly on the path to heaven where we, with you, can profess our love for him, para siempre (forever). Amen.

BLESSED ARE THE PURE IN HEART:
FOR THEY SHALL SEE GOD.

— MATTHEW 5:8

BLESSED MOTHER TERESA OF CALCUTTA

A sea of impoverished humanity suffers in the slums of the world—and we ask ourselves how one person can make a difference. Mother Teresa of Calcutta dedicated her life to showing us how big a difference a single human being can make. Many affectionately refer to her as the saint of the gutters.

Born in Skopje, Macdeonia (then Yugoslavia) in 1910, Agnes Gonxha Bojaxhiu was the daughter of an Albanian farmer named Nikolle Bojaxhiu and his wife Drana Bernai. Both parents were devout Catholics. When Agnes was nine years old, her father died from poisoning after attending a political meeting. His death united the family as nothing else. By the age of 12, Agnes already had an inner stirring that was calling her to a missionary vocation helping the poor.

When she was 18 years old, Agnes was accepted into the Order of the Sisters of our Lady of Loreto (also called the Irish Ladies), an Irish religious community founded in the sixteenth century to do missionary work in Calcutta, India. In September 1928, Agnes was provisionally admitted to the order. She journeyed to Dublin, where she was immersed in English-language studies before being sent to India.

Lived–A.D. 1910–1997
Beatified–October 19, 2003

She took initial vows as a nun on May 24, 1931 and took the name Teresa in honor of the saint she deeply admired, Saint Thérèse of Lisieux. In 1937, she professed final vows as a Sister of Our Lady of Loreto. For the next decade and a half, Mother Teresa taught at Calcutta's Saint Mary's High School, which was run by the Sisters of Our Lady of Loreto. She eventually became the director of studies at the school.

Beyond the walls of the convent, however, Mother Teresa witnessed incredible misery and suffering. Moved by this poverty, she received permission to leave the convent and work in the slums. In 1946, Sister Teresa set out to make a difference in the lives of the poorest of Calcutta's poor.

Initially, she had no funds to work with, but that didn't stop her from starting a school for homeless children. They would simply meet in an open-air space. Soon there were many helping hands, including volunteers from the slums and monetary donations from church organizations and various city officials.

In 1949, the first of many former students of Mother Teresa joined her in her holy work. These students became the foundation of an order founded the following year when, in October 1950, Mother Teresa received permission to establish her religious order, The Missionaries of Charity. Its mandate was for the sisters to love and care for those people who had no one else to care about them.

Teresa's religious community, initially made up of 10 women, now numbers over 1,000 sisters and brothers in India. Many are professionally trained as doctors, social workers, and nurses to serve the indigent in the slums as well as do relief work associated with natural catastrophes.

On the feast day of Mary Immaculate in 1952, a home called Nirmal Hriday (Home of the Pure Heart) was opened in the heart of Calcutta to care for the dying and destitute. Mother Teresa went on to spearhead children's homes, homes for the dying, a leper colony, medical clinics, a mother-house convent for her sisters, and projects in the slums—in all, more than 50 relief projects in India. In addition, her order is involved in outreach programs in other third-world countries, including Latin America, Asia, and Africa.

Mother Teresa's dedication to championing the needs of the poor and her selfless work with the dying have stirred consciences around the globe. Branches of her order can now be found in Ireland, Italy, the United States, and the United Kingdom.

During her lifetime, Mother Teresa received many awards, including the Padna Sri, or Order of the Lotus, from the Indian Government in 1962 and also the Magsaysay Award, presented by the SEATO organization of nations in Southeast Asia. She received the Pope John XXIII Peace Prize in 1971, the Nehru Prize in 1972, and in 1979 the Nobel Peace Prize as well as the Balzan Prize for promoting peace and brotherhood among nations. Of her awards, she said that she didn't feel she deserved them but had accepted them to acknowledge the kindness of those who gave the awards and to benefit from what such awards could mean in terms of helping the poor and the lepers.

Twice in 1993 Mother Teresa collapsed from her failing heart. Recovering somewhat, she again suffered in 1996 when she fractured her collarbone after falling out of bed. Four months later, she came down with malarial fever, which in turn aggravated her heart condition. Many followers begged her to slow down, to which she replied that she had all of eternity in which to rest. Then, in September 1997, Mother Teresa collapsed from a fatal heart attack.

On the first anniversary of Mother Teresa's death, an Indian woman experienced a miraculous healing from an abdominal tumor that disappeared overnight after the Sisters of Charity prayed to the Holy Mother, asking for her intervention. This was the miracle needed to qualify Mother Teresa for beatification. Pope John Paul waived the normal five-year waiting period, allowing the canonization cause for Mother Teresa to proceed. Her beatification ceremony on October 19, 2003, many believe, is the last measured step to sainthood.

Yet Mother Teresa is already revered as such. Her tomb in Calcutta continues to be a shrine for pilgrims who say they are receiving grace and strength. Ironically, her heart, which was so weak all of her life and especially in later years, became an indestructible chalice that held a magnificent love for everyone, even those that others could not bear to look upon. ✙

WAYS TO HONOR AND INVOKE THE BLESSINGS OF MOTHER TERESA OF CALCUTTA

✙ Share knowledge. You know how to do something that someone else doesn't. Almost everyone does. Think about sharing that knowledge with others who can't afford to take a class or buy a book or even a newspaper. Consider sponsoring a poor child, volunteering to be a Big Brother or Big Sister, or being a foster parent.

✙ Ask yourself what Mother Teresa would do if she could see the slums in your community or meet those living in your town, city, or village who have nothing. Emulate her example.

✙ What might you be able to do or give to help continue Mother Teresa's work? Do it. Contact the Sisters of Charity in the city or town closest to you. For example, in San Francisco they are located at 1596 Fulton Street, San Francisco, CA 94117.

✙ If you don't already have an altar, consider making a small one. Cover it with a cloth with three pinstripes of blue to symbolize Mother Teresa's sari—white for purity, and blue, the color most associated with our Mother Mary.

Prayer to the Blessed Mother Teresa of Calcutta

O Blessed Mother Teresa, who entered the sea of impoverished humanity to love those with nothing, not even hope, we honor you and your exemplary life. We pray for courage like yours to walk fearlessly into a world of unending challenges and tests with only the words and example of our Savior as a constant companion. In your exalted place in the kingdom of heaven, we beseech you to hear our prayers of petition for those in our midst who are living lives unseen, unnoticed, and unloved. May the Lord give us the strength, courage, and compassion to reach out and make a difference in those lives. May he inspire us to pull back the curtain of complacency and look deeply at our less fortunate brethren that we will not hesitate to help however, wherever, and whenever we can. Amen.

STRIKING DEEDS ARE FORBIDDEN ME. I CANNOT PREACH THE GOSPEL;
I CANNOT SHED MY BLOOD, BUT WHAT MATTER? MY BROTHERS DO IT FOR
ME, WHILE I, A LITTLE CHILD, STAY CLOSE BESIDE THE ROYAL THRONE,
AND I LOVE FOR THOSE WHO FIGHT. LOVE PROVES ITSELF BY DEEDS.

— SAINT THÉRÈSE OF LISIEUX

SAINT THÉRÈSE OF LISIEUX

That God hears and answers prayers is easier for some to believe than others. But in her loving, childlike approach to spirituality, Saint Thérèse of Lisieux understood and trusted the Lord's promise in John 16:23: "Whatsoever ye shall ask the Father in my name, he will give it [to] you."

She is often referred to as "the Little Flower," but her name at birth was Marie Francoise Thérèse Martin. The youngest of nine children, four of whom died in infancy, Marie was born in Aleçon, France on January 2, 1873. All nine children, including two boys, shared the same first name, Marie (or Mary).

Marie's mother died when Marie was four. Her father moved the family to Lisieux, where his late wife's relatives lived. Marie grew into a beautiful teenager with a fervent love for God, and she wasted no time declaring her intention to become a saint. Marie and her three sisters would all become nuns, and although Marie was the youngest, she was the third to enter the convent. She was only 15 when the bishop gave her special permission to become a Carmelite nun at Lisieux. She took the religious name of Theresa of the Infant Jesus but was later given permission to add the words "and of the Holy Face" in remembrance of Jesus' suffering.

In the cloistered convent, she lived a life devoted to tedious chores and a regimen of prayer. Her path to holiness was simple and direct. She received spiritual sustenance and insight from heartfelt prayer and devotional reading of Scripture and from the writings of holy persons like Saint John of the Cross, Teresa of Àvila, and Francis de Sales.

When she suffered her first hemorrhage on Good Friday, April 3, 1896 and was diagnosed with tuberculosis, her hope of serving as a missionary in Hanoi, in what was then French Indochina but is now North Vietnam, was dashed. The abbess, who was her sister, made a suggestion that Thérèse write an account of her life. Although her body was wracked with fever and nausea and the tuberculosis had reduced her to an emaciated state and caused gangrene, Thérèse completed *The Story of a Soul* just before her death. Her last words were about love of God, and moments before her passing, her eyes, which had been gazing beyond the statue of Mary beside her bed, filled with a light of supernatural joy.

Lived–A.D. 1873–1897
Canonized–May 17, 1925
Feast day–October 1
Patron saint of France, Russia, aviators, florists, and missionaries

I choose everything; my God, I do not want to be a Saint by halves. I am not afraid to suffer for Your sake; I only fear doing my own will, so I give it to You and choose everything You will.

—SAINT THÉRÈSE OF LISIEUX, 1997

On September 30, 1897, after weeks of tortuous physical suffering, Thérèse died at the age of 24. *The Story of a Soul*, with an initial printing of 20,000, was circulated first to the Carmelite convents and then to a wider public. Later, the book was translated into several languages and became one of the best-selling books of the twentieth century, selling millions of copies in more than 38 languages. It is still being sold and read today.

Saint Thérèse promised to do "good on Earth as long as there are souls to be saved." She also said that after her death, she would rain roses from heaven, and it is believed that the sight or scent of roses is a sign that God has granted one's prayerful petition. (Saint Thérèse of Lisieux, 1997)

I am only a very little soul, who can offer only very little things to our Lord.

—SAINT THÉRÈSE OF LISIEUX, 1997

As news spread of countless miracles—of healing and favors granted—attributed to her intercession, the Little Flower's popularity grew. The long mandatory wait for canonization to begin was waived in her case. She was beatified in 1923 and canonized on May 17, 1925. Pope John Paul II named her a Doctor of the Church in 1997, making her the third of only three women, in a group that also includes 33 men, to be so named in the history of the church. ✙

WAYS TO HONOR AND INVOKE THE BLESSINGS OF SAINT THÉRÈSE OF LISIEUX

✙ Allocate some time each day for the devotional reading of Scripture and then pray for understanding. Be still. Expect his response. Know that you are a child of the loving Father. Have confidence that he hears and answers your prayers, just as he hears and answers the prayers of his saints.

✙ Weave a garland of flowers and offer it with prayers to God, or place fresh roses in a beautiful cut-glass vase in your home and let them remind you of Saint Thérèse of Lisieux's promise "to let fall from heaven a shower of roses." Saint Thérèse loved flowers, and when she was a little girl, she would weave them into garlands for her altar.

✝ Make a rose-scented candle (remembering that traditionally altar candles were made of more than 51 percent beeswax). Place it on a table scattered with fresh rose petals and light it before praying Saint Thérèse's novena. Have a priest bless your candle.

✝ Offer to do some humble or menial task for your church, your neighbor, or a loved one.

✝ Regularly read passages from *The Autobiography of Saint Thérèse of Lisieux: The Story of a Soul* and also *Maurice and Thérèse: The Inspiring Letters Between Thérèse of Lisieux and a Struggling Young Priest*. As you read, ask yourself how you can become a more loving and spiritual person.

Novena to Saint Thérèse of Lisieux

Saint Thérèse of the Child Jesus, during your short life on earth you became a mirror of angelic purity, of love strong as death, and of wholehearted abandonment to God. Now that you rejoice in the reward of your virtue, turn your eyes of mercy upon me, for I put all my confidence in you.

Obtain for me the need to keep my heart and mind pure and clean like your own, and to abhor sincerely whatever may in any way tarnish the glorious virtue of purity, so dear to our Lord.

Most gracious Little Rose Queen, remember your promises of never letting any request made to you go unanswered, of sending down a shower of roses, and of coming down to earth to do good. Full of confidence in your power with the Sacred Heart, I implore your intercession in my behalf and beg of you to obtain the request I so ardently desire. (Mention your request.)

Holy little Thérèse, remember your promise to do good upon the earth and to shower down your roses on those who invoke you. Obtain for me from God the graces I hope for from his infinite goodness. Let me feel the powers of your prayers in every need. Give me consolation in all the bitterness of this life, and especially at the hour of death, that I may be worthy to share eternal happiness with you in heaven. Amen.

Recite this novena nine times in a row for nine days in a row.

—CALAMARI AND DIPASQUA, 1999

THEREFORE, MY BELOVED BRETHREN, BE YE STEADFAST, UNMOVEABLE,
ALWAYS ABOUNDING IN THE WORK OF THE LORD, FORASMUCH
AS YE KNOW THAT YOUR LABOUR IS NOT IN VAIN IN THE LORD.

—1 CORINTHIANS: 15:58

SAINT VINCENT DE PAUL

Most Americans are very good about giving of themselves to help their favorite charities—whether it's a marathon bike ride to raise money for leukemia, a five-kilometer walk to generate funds for the American Heart Association, or a celebrity silent auction to help fund research for HIV/AIDS. We do our part, write it off at tax time, and go on with our lives. How many of us ask how much time proportionally we spend on charity work versus how much time we spend on everything else in our lives.

Some individuals, however, are driven to do more, to give more, and to keep on doing and giving. Saint Vincent de Paul was such a person. His vision prescribed a way for charities to be efficient and effective. We can only marvel at his organizational skills and the methodology behind his charities, which are still "giving" and "doing" today.

Vincent was born in 1581 into a family of peasants in southwest France (Gascony) in the village of Pouy. The family lived off its farm. There were six children in all—four sons and two daughters.

Vincent was educated by Franciscans and later attended Toulouse University. He was considered very intelligent, charismatic, and deeply devoted to God. When he was a mere 19 years old, Vincent was ordained a priest. He subsequently became a court chaplain.

The facts about the next section of his life, often included in biographies by hagiographers and other writers, are in dispute: namely, that he was taken captive during a boat trip from Marseilles to Narbonne in 1605 and spent two years in Tunisia as a slave. He escaped, so the stories go, by rowboat with his third owner, whom he had converted to Christianity, and the two landed in Provence in April 1607. From there, Vincent went to Rome, where scholars do seem to agree he stayed for a year.

He then went to Paris, where he met and joined a group of priests whose leader was Pierre de Bérulle (who would later become a cardinal). Vincent's next move was to Clichy to become a parish priest. In 1612, he took a position tutoring the children of the wealthy and powerful de Gondi family. Philip de Gondi was the count of Joigny, and Madame de Gondi, in need of a spiritual advisor and confessor, turned to Vincent.

Lived—A.D. 1581–1660
Canonized—1737
Feast day—September 27
Patron saint of charities

During the 12 years he held this position with the family, Vincent was able not only to serve the family as chaplain but also to work as a parish priest at Châtillon-les-Dombes, ministering to the poor and the sick, including orphaned children, hungry families, feeble old people, oppressed labors, and prisoners. Here, he developed a vision of charitable groups or communities of like-minded people who would take an active role in caring for those who could not care for themselves. Members of these groups would dedicate themselves to helping the needy and poor in small villages and towns.

The first such group, which came into being in 1617, comprised women who called themselves the Servants of the Poor. Within three months, Vincent had written their rule and gotten it approved by the archbishop of Lyon.

Thereafter, Vincent established many *charités*—both for men and for women. He went on to found the Filles de Charité, or Daughters of Charity, who would minister to the sick and do the work that the older, middle-class women of his charities could not do.

In 1633, Vincent and a widow named Louise de Marillac, who later would be canonized and declared the patron saint of social workers, decided it would be appropriate to offer some kind of training to the young girls involved with the Daughters of Charity. They considered the Daughters of Charity to be an order without vows or convent (an "unenclosed" order) and their work of caring for the sick to be a living prayer. The Holy See approved the new order in 1668. Louise de Marillac was named its first superior.

In ensuing years, Vincent endured several bouts of serious illness, eventually becoming physically incapacitated and unable to walk. On September 27, 1660, he died at the age of 80. He was beatified in 1729 and canonized in 1737 by pope Clement XII. Pope Leo XIII, in 1885, named him the patron saint of all works of charity. In 1833, Frederick Ozanam established a lay confraternity in keeping with Vincent's vision and called it the Society of Saint Vincent de Paul.

To date, biographies about the life of this saint number roughly 400. It is worth noting that Vincent spelled his name Vincent Depaul, for to spell his surname as de Paul implied nobility that he would not claim, having been born into a peasant family. ✠

WAYS TO HONOR AND INVOKE THE BLESSINGS OF SAINT VINCENT DE PAUL

☩ Clean out your closets and give the best items to your local Saint Vincent de Paul thrift shop.

☩ Make time to do a little self-examination each day and make a loving correction.

☩ Form your own family charity. Get children, relatives, and friends involved in a project to help raise funds or acquire items (cans of food, clothing, or medicines) needed by the poor. Don't wait until your children are grown to teach them charity and concern for others.

☩ Charitable acts begin at home. Undertake a prayerful period during which you ask the Lord to take complete possession of your soul. Ask him to teach you to let go of earthly desires and material pursuits. Pray for his guidance. Ask him to bless you with a deep desire to help others in your immediate family and in the larger family of your community and the world. Give him enough time during this prayerful meditation to impregnate your soul, heart, and mind with divinely inspired ideas for charity.

☩ Buy a book of spiritual poetry. Choose any line that piques your interest or a phrase that opens your heart. Write that line on a piece of paper and allow the words to lead you forward into creating a new poem. Keep a journal of each piece of poetry you write on any spiritual topic. During times in your life when you feel far from your "spiritual "center," re-read these poems and allow them to pull you inward.

✠✠✠✠✠✠✠✠✠✠✠✠✠✠✠✠✠✠✠✠✠✠✠

Prayer to Saint Vincent de Paul

Noble Saint Vincent de Paul, beloved servant of the poor, may we follow your example and do good works among those whom society has abandoned, enslaved, or forgotten. Inspire us to feed the hungry, to love a child, to provide comfort and medicine to the sick, to clothe those whose garments are threadbare, and to offer hope and our Lord's words to all who need respite. Pray for us to our beloved God that we may commit ourselves selflessly to doing the same charitable acts that you did all your life, and intercede with him that we may have the favor of his guidance and strength and love upon this important and meaningful work. Amen.

✠✠✠✠✠✠✠✠✠✠✠✠✠✠✠✠✠✠✠✠✠✠✠

SOURCES QUOTED IN THIS BOOK

Calamari, Barbara, and Sandra DiPasqua (1999), *Novena, The Power of Prayer*, Penguin Studio.

Churchill, Winston (1962), *The Birth of Britain*, Volume 1 of History of the English Speaking Peoples, Dodd, Mead & Co.

Ford-Grabowsky, Mary (2002), editor, *Sacred Voices, Essential Women's Wisdom through the Ages*, Harper San Francisco.

Ghezzi, Bert (2000), *Voices of the Saints, A Year of Readings*, an Image Book.

Glenstal Abbey (2001), *The Glenstal Book of Prayer, A Benedictine Prayer Book*, Limerick, Ireland, The Liturgical Press.

Lelen, Rev. J. M. (1997), translator, *The Confessions of Saint Augustine*, revised translation, Catholic Book Publishing.

Lovasik, Rev. Lawrence G., S.V.D. (2000), *A Treasury of Novenas*, Catholic Book Publishing Company.

Philip Lief Group, Inc., The (2003), *Saintly Support, A Prayer for Every Problem*, Andrews McMeel Publishing.

Rejnis, Ruth (2001), *The Everything Saints Book, Discover the Lives of the Saints Throughout History*, Adams Media.

Saint Catherine of Genoa (online), *The Life and Doctrine of Saint Catherine of Genoa*, Christian Classics Ethereal Library at Calvin College.

Saint Catherine of Siena (1974), "A Treatise of Prayer," in *The Dialogue of the Seraphic Virgin Saint Catherine of Siena*, translated by Algar Thorold, Tan Books and Publishers, Inc.

Saint Teresa of Ávila (1997), *Praying with Saint Teresa*, compiled by Battistina Capalbo, Wm. B. Eerdmans Publishing Co.

Saint Thérèse of Lisieux (1997), *The Story of a Soul*, Tan Publishers

Thigpen, Paul (2001), *A Dictionary of Quotes from the Saints*, Charis Books, Servant Publications.

BIBLIOGRAPHY

Altemose, Charlene. *What You Should Know about Mary.* Liguori: Liguori Publications, 1998.

Augustine. *The Confessions of St. Augustine.* Revision of the translation of Rev. J. M. Lelen, Ph.D. Totowa: Catholic Book Publishing, 1997.

Calamari, Barbara and Sandra DiPasqua. *Novena, the Power of Prayer.* New York: Penguin Studio, member of Penguin Putnam, Inc., 1999.

Cavallini, Guiliana. *Saint Martin de Porres, Apostle of Charity.* Rockford: Tan Books and Publishers, Inc., 2000.

Compton-Hernandez, Maria. *The Catholic Mother's Resource Guide, a Resource Listing of Hints and Ideas for Practicing and Teaching the Faith.* Goleta: Queenship Publishing Company, 2002.

Deen, Edith. *All the Women of the Bible.* New York: HarperCollins Publishers, Inc.

Dues, Greg. *Catholic Customs and Traditions, a Popular Guide.* Mystic: Twenty-Third Publications, 2000.

Farmer, David. *Oxford Dictionary of Saints.* Fourth edition. Oxford: Oxford University Press, 1997.

Ford-Grabowsky, Mary, editor. *Sacred Voices: Essential Women's Wisdom through the Ages.* New York: HarperCollins Publishers, Inc., 2002.

Fox, Matthew. *Illuminations of Hildegard of Bingen.* Text by Hildegard of Bingen with commentary by Matthew Fox. Rochester: Bear & Company, 2002.

Gesualda of the Holy Spirit, Sister. *St. Theresa, the Little Flower.* Margaret M. Repton, translator. Boston: Daughters of St. Paul, 1973.

Ghezzi, Bert. *Voices of the Saints, a Year of Readings.* New York: Doubleday, Division of Random House, Image Book, 2000.

Holböck, Ferdinand, and Michael J. Miller, editors. *New Saints and Blesseds of the Catholic Church: Blesseds and Saints Canonized by Pope John Paul II During the Years 1979-1983.* San Francisco: Ignatius Press, 2000.

Johnson, Kevin Orlin, Ph.D. *Rosary Mysteries, Meditations and the Telling of the Beads.* Dallas: Pangaeus Press, 1996.

Klein, Peter. *Catholic Source Book, a Comprehensive Collection of Information about the Catholic Church.* Dubuque: Harcourt Religion Publishers, 2000.

Lovasik, Lawrence G. *Treasury of Novenas.* Totowa: Catholic Book Publishing, 2000.

McBrien, Richard D. *The Lives of the Saints: From Mary and St. Francis of Assisi to John XXIII and Mother Teresa.* New York: HarperSanFrancisco, HarperCollins Publishers, Inc., 2001.

Martin, John. *Roses, Fountains, and Gold: The Virgin Mary in History, Art, and Apparition.* San Francisco: Ignatius Press, 1998.

Melloni, Javier, S. J. *The Exercises of St. Ignatius Loyola in the Western Tradition.* Leominster: Gracewing, 2000.

Rejnis, Ruth. *The Everything Saints Book.* Avon: Adams Media Corporation, 2001.

Sharma, Arvin, editor. *Women Saints in World Religions.* Albany: State University of New York Press, 2000.

Teresa, Mother, Becky Benenate, and Joseph Durepos, editors. *Mother Teresa, No Greater Love.* Novato: New World Library, 1997.

The Philip Lief Group, Inc. *Saintly Support: A Prayer for Every Problem.* Kansas City: Andrews McMeel Publishing, 2003.

Thérèse of Lisieux, Saint. *The Story of a Soul, The Autobiography of St. Therese of Lisieux.* Mother Agnes of Jesus, editor, and Michael Day, translator. Rockford: Tan Books and Publishers, Inc., 1997.

Thigpen, Paul. *A Dictionary of Quotes from the Saints.* Ann Arbor: Servant Publications, Charis Books, 2001.

Thorold, Algar, translator. *The Dialogue of the Seraphic Virgin Catherine of Siena.* Rockford: Tan Books and Publishers, Inc., 1974.

Walsh, Michael, editor. *Butler's Lives of the Saints.* New York: HarperCollins Publishers, Inc., 1991.

Walsh, William Thomas. *Saint Teresa of Ávila.* Rockford: Tan Books and Publishers, Inc. 1944.